The Amish
of Holmes County

- A Culture
- A Religion
- A Way Of Life

Published by:

Spectrum Publications
P.O. Box 8
409 N. Main St.
Orrville, Ohio, 44667
Phone: 330-682-2055
Fax: 330-683-2041

Copyright © 1996 by Spectrum Publications

All rights reserved. No part of this book may be reproduced in any form or by any electronic or mechanical means, including information storage and retrieval systems, without prior written permission from the publisher, except for brief passages quoted in a review.

Printed in the United States of America

ISBN 0-9654997-0-7

Dedicated to the memory of James A. Miller, 1952-1993, one of the authors whose work is included in this book.

Contents

Introduction .... Page 4
Section I — Who They Are
    An Amishman's personal expression .... Page 7
    Life in the slow lane .... Page 13
Section II — Some History
    The history of the Amish .... Page 25
    Not all Amish are the same .... Page 37
    Various orders live in harmony .... Page 45
    Mural portrays history of Amish .... Page 49
Section III — Customs & Traditions
    Buggies are plain, practical .... Page 55
    An account of a buggy ride .... Page 63
    Clothing sets them apart .... Page 67
    Amish quilts are works of art .... Page 73
    Late fall is the time for weddings .... Page 77
    A young couple talks about life .... Page 83
    Birthing center serves Amish well .... Page 87
    Friends, church provide insurance .... Page 95
    A barn-raising .... Page 101
    Church leaders chosen by lots .... Page 105
    Tragedy accepted as God's way .... Page 109
    Shunning used to guard culture .... Page 111
Section IV — Growing Up
    Separate schools serve Amish youth .... Page 125
    An Amish teacher describes school .... Page 131
    "City" teachers like the area, too .... Page 139
    Boys become men at age 14 .... Page 143
    Girls like to have fun, too .... Page 147
    There's time for games .... Page 151
Section V — Making A Living
    Rising land prices bring changes .... Page 155
    It hurts Amish to sell their land .... Page 161
    Families join to grow produce .... Page 165
    Catering helps family survive .... Page 169
    "Pie Mary" just keeps on baking .... Page 173
    Breaking horses is a way of life .... Page 179
    Many Amish are woodworkers .... Page 183
Section VI — Daily Tasks
    Here's what's cooking .... Page 187
    The iceman still cometh .... Page 193
    A family relates a typical day .... Page 197
    Dear diary .... Page 203
Section VII — Some Profiles
    Mose A. Kaufman .... Page 227
    Alma Kaufman .... Page 233
    Donald G. Beam .... Page 241
Section VIII — Conclusion
    Remembrance of things past .... Page 251
Section IX — Credits & Misc.
    Contributors .... Page 271
    Acknowledgments, for more information, maps .... Page 272

INTRODUCTION

By Jon Kinney, editor

Holmes County, Ohio, and portions of several counties surrounding it, is home to the largest concentration of Amish in the world.

Many people visiting the area for the first time may feel like they have stepped back into the 19th century.

The Amish — who disdain most of the modern conveniences of life that a majority of Americans couldn't live a week, let alone a lifetime, without — still rely on "horse power," not only to farm their fields, but also to take them here and there on daily errands and social occasions.

The Amish mode of dress also is distinctive. Whether or not their children should wear uniforms to school will never be an issue with the Amish. From youngsters to elders, it appears to outsiders that the Amish all dress uniformly.

But these are only surface manifestations of what sets the Amish apart from the rest of the world — or the "English," as they refer to anyone who is non-Amish. The Amish culture, religion and way of life have developed and evolved over three centuries. Their roots predate the automobile and electricity by more than two centuries. These hardy people have proven that cultures can adapt to modern technology but not be corrupted by it.

For the past six years, starting in 1991, the weekly newspaper that serves Holmes County, *The Holmes County Hub*, has produced an annual special section — "The Amish: A Culture, A Religion, A Way of Life" — that has attempted to provide its readers with a better understanding of their Amish neighbors. This special section, which also has been distributed throughout the state and beyond by Ohio's tourism department, has received numerous awards for its consistent excellence.

After the sixth special section was published in the spring of 1996, it was decided that a book should be produced that would contain the best work, in both words and photographs, from those six special sections.

This book will appeal to anyone who desires a better understanding of the Amish way of life. It will help explain why the Amish have been able to survive and prosper in spite of having cloistered themselves from much of life in the latter part of the 20th century.

In deciding which articles and photographs to include in this book, we attempted to put together a selection that would provide a comprehensive look at the Amish — from their long history down to their daily routines.

You will find that the Amish perspective is well-represented. From the first article, "An Amishman's Personal Expression," to the last, "Remembrance of Things Past," and some in between, we let Amish or former Amish speak for themselves.

All 38 articles contained in this book originally appeared in one of the special sections. Some have been edited for space considerations. People's names, ages and locations were accurate at the time the articles first were published. We have not updated, for example, the age of any individual.

Many of the photographs in this book also originally appeared in one of the special sections, although we have added some new ones. Photographs were selected with an eye toward illustrating both the articles and the Amish way of life in general.

We believe *The Amish of Holmes County* will, indeed, provide you with a greater understanding of the Amish culture, the Amish religion and the Amish way of life. And, perhaps, even our own lives.

SECTION I
WHO THEY ARE

An Amishman's Personal Expression

By David Schlabach

If you ask us Amish people about the way we live, you might often receive a somewhat unsatisfactory answer. But that response is not an evasive one, or a gesture of rudeness.

We might be inclined to ask in return, "Why do you want to know?" before giving any reasonable explanations concerning our lifestyle. We might even be tempted to ask, "Why should the Amish way of life be important to anyone other than the Amish people?"

For a long time, people regarded our Amish way of life as strange and peculiar, somehow odd and restrictive, undesirable, and sometimes, amusing. In the past few years, however, so much has changed. We haven't, or not very much, comparatively. But the world has. Both in relation to itself and in relation to

us. Amish institutions and practices have even been suggested as effective models for solving many contemporary social problems.

For example, when unchecked economic growth and expansion brings in its train social and ecological devastations, Amish frugality can come to be seen not as pointless eccentricity, but as essential virtue. Or when American agriculture draws fire because of its dependence on petroleum fuels and fertilizers, its promotion of soil erosion and lack of crop diversity, Amish agricultural practices become an ecologically sound and proven alternative. Small-scale, family operated farms tilled with horses provide more than nostalgic scenes for tourists.

They're a central means of support for many Amish families, all without threat to our environment or the eliminating of precious resources.

To many people we've become a symbol of the (re)discovery of the simple life. Some sociologists and naturalists see a vital link between the Amish and ecology. Other social critics applaud the Amish way and the Amish family as a prototype for what our future as a nation must include.

However, besides our sense of community, use of resources and a certain independence, beyond all the kind and indeed appreciated words that might be said in our behalf, we, within, sense our greater strength in a strong and convincing sense of purpose.

One expression of that sense of purpose is that we don't subject ourselves to everyone else telling us what we need. We have little use for today's self-improvement seminars, self-actualization workshops, or books on how to improve your figure, run a marathon, make love, get rich or impress people.

Neither do we destroy our own originality or creativeness by being dictated to and endlessly entertained by the fantasy world of sports and theater. A simple process of eliminating TVs, radios and other electronic distractions, and encouraging family and community cohesiveness and interactions accomplishes this.

In many ways the Amish are more liberated than those in society who feel compelled and pressured to excel at whatever the latest expert dictates. Why and how? Because of an unwavering standard by which we dismiss much of today's reigning culture. And it is also, finally, this unwavering standard that leads us to think that to use us as a model for others is likely misguided and, perhaps, foolhardy.

What is missing in most books, lectures and articles on the Amish is the realization that our greatest sense of purpose is fundamentally religious. It is the sense of responding to God's will for man. We are not bound together by mere ecological or humanistic concerns. Neither are we primarily an ethnic group.

One is not born Amish, in a complete sense.

Instead, each Amish man and woman must elect to become Amish by being baptized in the church. Our Anabaptist heritage was founded on the principle of choice. This primacy of religion over ethnicity also means that individuals raised in non-Amish families can become Amish if they are willing to live by the rules and are sincere in their religious convictions.

Adherence to Amish practice, however, without an understanding of its religious basis is bordering on meaningless. It also becomes a danger within the Amish culture to become such without the proper exercising of spiritual values. Therefore, to use the Amish as a model without accepting the spiritual is like separating the secular from the sacred in human behavior.

To take but several examples. The Amish one-room schoolhouse could be viewed, and is in some quarters, as a potential model for progressive education. Its true form, however, is a direct expression of the goal of Amish parochial education: "To prepare for usefulness by preparing for eternity."

Or when Amish congregations permit the rental of cars and drivers for transportation, yet at the same time the ownership of motor vehicles is prohibited — this is because the constant use of cars would automatically change our family structures. Such distinctions only make sense within the context of a unique historical and religious setting.

Another illustration is in our marriages and our understanding of fidelity and commitment. To be married to a single partner for life is a blessing to any family, community and society, but the Amish regard and pursue such a position not merely for its social benefits, lack of confusion and security to the children, but simply by believing that this is God's order and will for mankind.

While most of society focuses on a large structure or church building to worship in, the Amish continue to attend services held in each other's homes. This not only reduces the high cost of a special building used primarily for a singular purpose, but it avoids the separating of a home and/or special place of worship. Preparing for services becomes a family and neighborhood event.

Since the Bible is acknowledged as the ultimate truth, guide and divine authority, we find it safe to apply its principles to determine how to live godly and upright lives. All cultural practices must also be measured in that light — that they either find harmony in or enhance scriptural understanding.

A local Amish minister has said that he receives numerous letters inquiring how to become Amish. What most of the writers are after though, he has discovered, is Amish practices minus the beliefs: "They don't want to know about our commitment to Jesus Christ, which is the basis for everything we do."

His replies to the would-be Amish boldly state that commitment. And perhaps, not surprisingly, most of the seekers lose interest. Yet we continue to feel that it is our mission to exhibit Christian behavior in every part of our lives, and our lifestyle is a silent witness to this faith.

In our lifestyle, we have attracted much attention, but in our faith we have been more avoided and less attractive. Perhaps this will change also.

Editor's note: Portions of the above article were adapted from an article originally written by Professor Mark Olshan. That article appeared in "Christianity Today" in 1983.

It's common for church services to be held in a barn.

LIFE IN THE SLOW LANE

By L. Edward Purcell

Motoring over the crest of a ridge in Holmes County, you suddenly may be confronted by a pair of horse-drawn buggies racing toward you side-by-side in a seemingly reckless effort to determine who owns the fastest horse flesh.

This is the heart of Old Order Amish country, and horses and horse-drawn vehicles are everywhere — clogging the back roads, filling up parking lots in town. When you drive the country lanes, it's inevitable that you will share the roadway with Amish-filled buggies or iron-wheeled wagons, the latter pulled by huge draft horses.

Visiting motorists may be nervous at first, but they get used to such equine traffic. It is all a part of the slower pace here: Eyes and ears tell you to relax and enjoy an authentic slice of what America was like be-

fore the automobile, the telephone, the airplane and the computer.

The area is densely populated by members of the Old Order Amish religious sect, whose Swiss ancestors broke from the Mennonite Church in Europe more than 300 years ago. They since have followed their own religious beliefs and have been labeled the "plain people" because of the simplicity of their life and their conspicuous rejection of much of modern technology.

The Old Order Amish first settled in Holmes County at the beginning of the 19th century, and in the years since, especially during this century, their numbers have exploded. Now, they virtually fill Holmes County and spill over into adjacent Wayne, Coshocton, Tuscarawas, Knox and Ashland counties. This section of Ohio contains the world's largest Amish settlement, with perhaps as many as 30,000 Amish people placed into the relatively small area.

"We hardly have elbow room," one Amishman says.

Holmes County is about 60 miles south of Cleveland in the center of a triangle formed by Interstate highways 70, 71 and 77. It takes less than two hours to drive here from Cleveland or Columbus, and about an hour from Akron.

For mile after mile, the farmsteads are uncluttered white frame houses surrounded by flower beds and

long clotheslines from which may hang beautiful, hand-sewn quilts. The Amish homes, which lack electricity and even central heating, are flanked by at least one multi-story barn large enough to accommodate numbers of horses and Holstein cows. Windmills power the pumps that supply water for people and animals.

The area has seen little commercial exploitation. Although the number of non-Amish tourist enterprises is growing in the small central towns of Berlin, Walnut Creek and Sugarcreek, the overall effect is as yet muted. The region seems virtually unspoiled when compared to such better-known Amish hot spots as Lancaster County, Pa.

A foggy morning drive

Visitors to Holmes County will find the Amish easy to spot. Men wear only black or dark blue clothing without zippers and seldom are seen without their signature broad-brimmed hats — black in the fall and winter, light straw in spring and summer. They sport untrimmed, mustache-less beards. The women's unshorn hair always is caught up under white, long-laced caps, and their dresses are plain, although on non-church days women's clothing is more colorful, more of a contrast to the drab attire of the men folk. Amish children are dressed like their elders, and to most outsiders' eyes appear to be immensely endearing miniature adults.

Perhaps the most distinctive practice of the Old Order Amish, however, is the nearly complete reliance on horses for farming and travel. They believe that ownership and operation of automobiles is contrary to their way of life.

Plan for a stay of several days. In Amish country you can find lodging ranging from basic to fairly luxurious, none of it expensive. Then strike out on day trips, following no agenda.

You first might want to tour a few commercial sites in the towns to pick up maps, but leave the heavy shopping until later. There are tourist attractions near Berlin and Walnut Creek billed as Amish farms that are not authentic, but that feature buggy rides and animal petting zoos for the kids.

As for dining, many visitors come armed with the notion that Amish eat well, and most of the restaurants in the area advertise what they call "Amish-style" cooking. In fact, when at home the Amish tend to eat simply except for special feasts, and most of their cooking is plain country fare designed to feed large families without much cash outlay.

Outsiders are likely to see entire Amish families at local restaurants, as eating out is as much a treat for them as for the non-Amish. The McDonald's in Sugarcreek and Millersburg, as well as the Burger King in Berlin, are three of the few fast-food outlets in the country to have hitching rails for buggies in the parking lot.

The Amish in Holmes County and surrounding counties are almost uniformly friendly to outsiders. If you treat them with respect and honest interest and not as curiosities, they are likely to receive you with grace and courtesy. One caveat: The Amish do not like to be photographed and will not pose for pictures. Visitors who observe these rules will find many Amish willing, and in some cases eager, to talk of the unusual way of life.

Even though the Amish often have been portrayed as stern and forbidding, in fact they are gregarious people and are immensely fond of what they call "visiting." Far from being dour workaholics, most Amish are happy to take time away from chores to

chat with outsiders.

The Amish love to travel, for example, and are curious to learn more about other parts of the country. They also are interested in discussing almost any aspect of agriculture or small business manufacturing, and they often probe visitors for information.

Much of what you see when you journey along the back roads induces a vague sense that you have entered a time-warp. First, there are so many more farms than we are accustomed to seeing. Amish holdings are limited in size by the number of acres one family can manage with only horses, so a single hilltop vista in Holmes County may reveal a dozen farms.

Moreover, the Amish practice of crop rotation induces them to break up their farms into many small fields. The result creates a quilt-like pattern that is striking to eyes more accustomed to endless row crops. The appearance of the very soil itself is distinct, as much of the land has felt only the hooves of draft horses. The undulating fields look soft and yielding in a way land worked by tractors cannot.

Ancient-looking, horse-drawn implements work the fields, and Amish people use their own muscle power for many of the basic tasks of farming. During the late-summer harvest, for example, it is normal to see entire Amish families in the fields hoisting sheaves of oats or barley on pitchforks — scenes that

might have been painted by Pieter Brueghel centuries ago.

In addition to the distinctive Amish farmsteads, visitors will drive past one-room schoolhouses, perhaps with children at play in the spacious schoolyards if the weather is good. These are private Amish schools that hew to the Amish belief that children should have no more than eighth-grade educations. A U.S. Supreme Court decision 20 years ago granted the Old Order Amish the right to keep their children out of public schools.

Keep a lookout for hand-lettered signs advertising produce or canned goods or specialty products. Many Amish families supplement their incomes by selling to neighbors and tourists. What better way to meet Amish people than to stop off for a jar of apple butter, a pot of honey, a jug of local maple syrup or handmade wooden crafts?

The Amish also sell more sophisticated products. There are several small Amish-run enterprises around the region, such as the Hickory Rocker Shop southeast of Millersburg, which specializes in making and selling a distinctive Amish style of rustic hickory furniture. Amish craftsmen gather the wood, shape the pieces and assemble the chairs. Amish women often apply the finishes. The rockers are usually less than $200.

During a visit to the Hickory Rocker Shop, the 75-

year-old retired farmer who runs the enterprise stopped sanding to talk as soon as it became apparent that a leisurely visit was in the offing. He detailed the increasing difficulty of finding high-grade hickory in the region and lamented the need to go farther away to get his raw materials. His comments were punctuated by the gentle "swish-swish-swish" of his wife's brush as she applied shellac to a finished chair. When teased about a recent back-road buggy race in which he and his wife nearly took a spill, the elderly furniture-maker responded with a twinkle. "Well," he said, "I like to have a little fun."

There are many other points of interest in the tiny villages and small towns such as Charm, Millersburg, Bunker Hill, Trail, Benton, Mount Hope, Kidron and others. For example, you might enjoy a stop at one of the so-called "bulk stores" that cater to the Amish. These combination groceries and general stores harken to an earlier time, and visitors can rub shoulders with Amish shoppers.

Even if you own no horses and need no new outdoor footgear, it's worth a visit to the Amish-run harness and boot shop in tiny New Bedford, just to inhale the aroma of leather that saturates the atmosphere.

At any of your stops, you might ask if there's to be a barn-raising anywhere in the area. Don't get your hopes up because it is a rare event, but if you are lucky, you will see what is probably the biggest public event for the Amish.

The spirit of cooperation runs strong among the Amish, and nowhere is it more visible than at barnraisings. As many as 700 men may be working while the women cook and the children watch. Offer your help, and you may be invited to partake of the big meal when the work is done.

A sure way to get a close-up view of the Amish is to attend local farm sales. Old-fashioned public sales are held in a different village each weekday, and Amish farmers flock in to buy, sell and trade. Wednesday livestock sales at Mount Hope or the famous Friday horse sale at Sugarcreek attract hundreds of local Amish. The parking lots surrounding the sale barn are choked with open-air peddlers hawking everything from hand tools to used paperback books, and there are lines of horse-drawn wagons waiting to unload livestock into the holding pens.

Inside the huge barn, the worn, dusty wooden benches of the sales amphitheater fill with Amishmen as the start of the sale approaches, and the air is thick with the sound of the Amish "Dutch" dialect (actually a dialect of German similar to that spoken in Pennsylvania; don't be confused by the many references to things "Dutch" in the area; it is all really German.) Usually there are lots of Amish children at the sales, sitting shyly with their fathers but showing

clearly that this is an exciting trip for them.

Just remember to keep your hands at your sides during the bidding or you may inadvertently buy the beginnings of your own Holstein dairy herd.

After you've spent a couple of days touring the real Amish countryside, you might visit the many shops in Berlin, Walnut Creek and Sugarcreek. The main highways through these towns are lined with stores, selling a very wide variety of merchandise, some of it authentic Amish-related or Amish-made goods, and some pure tourist puff.

The best buys probably are the quilts made by Amish women. You likely will have seen quilts hanging on the front-yard clotheslines of Amish farms during your rambles, and a group of buggies parked at one house during a weekday probably means an Amish quilting party is in session. The design and workmanship of local quilts are superb, and they can command fancy prices elsewhere in the country. When purchased at the source they are relatively inexpensive, some no more than a few hundred dollars. A good place to find genuine local Ohio Amish quilts is the Helping Hands Quilt Shop, a nonprofit co-op, off Main Street in Berlin.

Other interesting local products are various kinds of country-style food, including the renowned Trail Bologna (named after the nearby village of Trail), fresh cheeses manufactured locally from milk sup-

plied by Amish farmers, Amish-made dried noodles and fresh baked goods.

The thoughtful visitor to Ohio's Amish country, however, takes away something more valuable than handmade quilts and more nourishing than local foodstuffs. If you allow yourself to enter into the atmosphere of the place, you gain a perspective on modern life.

The simple beauty of the region and the distinctive lifestyle of the people combine to create an authentic rural enclave. Here a visitor may borrow — if only for a while — the slow-paced serenity of the Amish.

A group of Amish girls heads home for the day.

Section II
Some History

The History of the Amish

By Leroy Beachy

Spreading over the hills and valleys of Holmes County and extending across its boundaries into neighboring Coshocton, Tuscarawas, Stark and Wayne counties is today's largest continuous Amish community.

For thousands like myself, born of Amish parents and by choice a member of this faith, Holmes County is accounted as center of the earth and the Amish way of life as "The Normal Life." All other cultural patterns seem to us strange, and the territories beyond our own community appear as alien space, separating us from other Amish communities like our own throughout the nation and hemisphere.

But to the passers-by of another culture, we, in turn, seem strange, our community noticeably different. To such people arise questions such as: "Who are

these people?" "What are their beliefs?" and "How have they come to be?"

Basically, the Amish faith is an attempt at having one's life altered and ordered by the teachings of Jesus Christ. Ours is not the only attempt, and how well anyone is succeeding shall be ultimately revealed by the only faithful and true judge.

That age that is historically known as the Reformation gave birth to our denominational ancestry. When Ulrich Zwingli, a Swiss Reformation leader, decided to stop short of a total scriptural reforming of the church, a number of his supporters became dissatisfied with his methods.

Infant baptism and participation in war were two great issues that Zwingli refused to omit. As a result, the evening of Jan. 21, 1525, found a small gathering of zealous, young, university-trained men in counsel and prayer. During this meeting, "believer's (adult) baptism" was co-administered to those present, and it was this assembly that provided the nucleus of a new and fast-growing church that was soon to be severely persecuted and nicknamed Anabaptist.

The rapid spreading of the new faith from Switzerland throughout northern Europe disclosed an eagerness and desire for release from the grip of a church that, having sadly lost its way and having fallen from its original purity, was ". . . teaching for doctrine the commandments of men."

Because of their radical, down-to-the-root reforms at the expense of long-established practices, these Bible-believing people were considered heretical and dangerous by those "blind leaders of the blind" who were in control of the ecclesiastical and civil powers. Thus, for centuries, our forefathers suffered severe persecution and martyrdom at the hands of determined and affrighted authorities.

But the truth has a way of surviving and overcoming, and so it did in the hearts of those dedicated believers who kept the true faith, and by so doing, preserved it for each oncoming generation.

There occurred in the late 1600s in Switzerland and the adjoining Alsatian and Palatinate areas a series of incidents that gave birth both to the name "Amish" and to the establishment of certain patterns of discipline that have survived in the Amish churches to this day and are largely responsible for its historical distinctiveness of faith and practice.

It appears that the Bible-disciplinary Swiss Anabaptists, who had held out so valiantly, for so long, were suddenly weakening. The appearance of fashionable dress and beard-marring were but external evidence of a general laxity of former convictions.

Among those who sensed alarm was Jacob Amman, a young Alsatian bishop. Amman, fiery and spontaneous by nature, with a strong Bible-centered faith and apparently inspired by the writings of

Menno Simons, set about to affect a purifying revival and reform. And although reform efforts very seldom meet with wide approval, 20 of 22 Alsatian ministers supported his initial efforts, indicating Amman as having been a capable leader.

Amman's next move was to contact, by visit, the congregations of his homeland in Switzerland, where again those ministers first contacted approved of his ideals. However, he soon met a foe, aged Bishop Hans Reist. Reist, also an able and influential leader, may have thought that Amman's success would weaken his own venerable position. At least, he set about actively opposing him, soon turning Amman's Swiss supporters against him.

Amman, being a strong believer in the use of the "ban," as taught by Simons, then used this means against Reist and his active supporters to stem their opposition. However, Amman soon found himself and his followers banned by Reist in retaliation. And so with a double ban separating their fellowship and all attempts at reconciliation failing, the division eventually spread through all the Anabaptist communities in the Swiss, Alsatian and Palatinate areas.

Although the division is a sad historical fact, Amman's efforts were certainly not in vain, for he did instill a strong revival of Anabaptist ideals in his followers, and the opposing party also benefited greatly in later years by adopting some of his teach-

ings.

Among the issues at stake in the controversy were: a strict observance of the ban and "avoidance," as a scriptural instrument of maintaining biblical discipleship; communal foot-washing, which had either never before been practiced by the Swiss Anabaptists or else had been abandoned; the holding of communion twice a year rather than once, for the benefit of child-bearing women; disciplinary dress standards, to combat worldly fashion; and the non-marring of the beard.

That Amman was, in reality, a zealous reformer and revivalist, rather than a mere legalistic traditionalist, as he has too often been thought of, can be gathered from a statement that he once made in a letter written during the heat of the controversy. He wrote: ". . . we will not heed the counsel of men, long-established customs or current practices, if they are not founded on the word of God, for our faith shall be pure, undimmed and established solely on the word of God."

A Dutch Mennonite who observed the Amish in the early 1700s said of them: "They are a sturdy folk by nature, able to endure great hardships, with long, untrimmed beards, simple clothes, heavy shoes, shod with clumsy irons held on with large nails. They are very zealous in serving God with prayer and reading and in other ways, and were very sincere and open-

hearted in all they did."

Within a generation or two, Amish families began turning their faces to a new land of opportunity, America. Perhaps between 50 and 100 Amish families arrived here between the years 1730 and 1770. After this, because of a succession of wars, immigration fell to a trickle, and by the time it resumed in full, the persecution of European Anabaptists had practically

The Amish and their horses travel in all kinds of weather.

ended. There were, however, numerous immigrations to America during the 1800s, but the greater part of the present Amish population is of the 1730-1770 stock.

The early Amish immigrants, having landed at Philadelphia, made their way inland to the frontier along the Blue Mountains, where they remained unmolested until the Indian raids of 1757, in which several Amish families were attacked. This caused them to retreat into the safer areas of Berks County. Soon, some were moving westward to Lancaster County, and later on westward to Mifflin County.

In 1767, Amishman Christian Blauch left Berks County to settle in the raw wilderness of southwestern Pennsylvania — now Somerset County. Every year following, increasing numbers of his friends followed, so that by 1800, there were three thriving Amish settlements there.

These three Somerset County communities, in turn, provided the greatest percentage of Amish settlers for Holmes County, and a generation later for Indiana. Mifflin County gave a few pioneer families to Holmes County. Some also came here in the early years directly from their homes in Europe.

"Ohio fever" must have started running high in Somerset County in about 1810. Bishop Jacob Miller and his sons, Henry and Jacob Jr., had moved with their families the year before, bringing with them 21-

year-old Jonas Stutzman, a single man and nephew of Mrs. Jacob Miller Sr. While the Millers settled in the valley a mile east of present-day Sugarcreek, Stutzman found the fertile Walnut Creek valley to his liking and erected a cabin there in the summer of 1809.

Immigration began in earnest in the spring of 1810, when four young families moved in and settled around Stutzman's claim: the Jonas Millers, a mile to the east; the Christian Yoders, a mile west; the John Troyers, a mile north; and the Jacob Masts, immediately northwest. The Abraham and Christian Hershberger families came later in the year. The next year brought the: Beachys, Weavers, Schrocks, Zooks, Yoders, Schlabachs, Yutzys, Wengerds, Hostetlers, Kauffmans, Gingerichs and others.

Increased numbers came in 1818, when government land prices dropped from $2 to $1.25 an acre, and again in 1820, when a 160-acre quarter section could first be divided in half. By 1835, 25 years after settlement began, there were 250 taxable Amish families here, with more moving in every year. The area roughly bounded by present-day Sugarcreek, Baltic, Farmerstown, Becks Mills, Saltillo, Benton, Mount Hope, Winesburg and back to Sugarcreek was by then heavily settled by Amish.

By the 1840s, however, most eastern Amish moving west were going to Indiana. Second-generation

Holmes Countians also were moving out to find new settlements throughout Ohio, as well as to join the flow to Indiana, Illinois and points farther west.

As long as the church maintained its original level of spiritual purity, there was peace and harmony, but by the early 1900s, a spiritual breakdown was again in evidence, with harmful habits and practices coming in, which may have been caused by intermarriage and close intermingling on the frontier with other cultures. Friction developed between the careless and the concerned, causing serious unrest in the churches, which numerous ministers' meetings could not bring to an end.

Serious rifts continued. There was a growing liberal faction whose tastes again became evident with the adoption of fashionable dress and beard-shaving. The westernmost settlements were the most strongly subjected to this influence, and by 1900, fully two-thirds of the American Amish had taken a very liberal path and are now largely liberal Mennonites.

Soon after the middle of the century, there were divisions in various communities in several states concerning a number of issues, of which one was a certain mode of baptism, teaching that converts should be baptized in a stream. Those of Holmes County who followed this movement eventually joined the Mennonite Conference. It is of interest to notice that after those who were involved in the divi-

sion had all passed on, this peculiar mode of baptism was abandoned.

So far in the 1900s, the Amish church in Holmes County has been beset with departures in both directions. There have been a number of withdrawals to an ultra-conservatism, among which the chief articles

This is the tomb of Jonas Stutzman, the first Amish settler in the Walnut Creek area.

of division are degrees of "meidung" (the application of "ban" and "avoidance"), and minute personal appearance and dress standards. An equal number of groups of a more liberal persuasion have been formed that have adopted, in common, such innovations as Sunday School and church buildings, but are divided on regulation of the use of such culture-affecting inventions as the automobile, radio and television.

Those who have moved too far in this direction are usually no longer regarded as Amish, but rather Mennonite, and the precise dividing line is between those men who retain a consistent beard and those who shave. Those beyond are not included in the *Raber's Almanac* list of Amish church districts.

Those closer to the center of the Amish norm have in very recent years divided on such issues as farm tractors, telephones, electricity, Sunday school and especially concerning a more spiritual social program for the young folks.

Today, 150 years after the introduction of the Amish faith to this area, we have at least 17 non-intercommuning groups that stem from the original congregation.

In spite of our apparent weaknesses, there are, we hope, in each of these groups those who compose, in part, "The One True Church of Jesus Christ," and may these continue to abide in those noticeable

Christian characteristics that will continue to cause the passer-by to wonder and by this, draw his attention to the kingdom of God and its invitation to partake of its benefits, everlasting life in particular.

As these mailboxes show, several generations often live on the same farm.

Not All Amish Are the Same

By Jeanine Kendle

It is possible to distinguish at least 12 separate groups of Amish and Mennonites according to their affiliation with, or independence from, national religious conferences. While it is not always easy to differentiate between one and another of the middle groups, there is an unmistakable cleavage between the extremes.

Practically all Mennonites use the Dortrecht Confession of Faith of 1632. The distinguishing marks, however, between one group and another are in the interpretation of the cardinal doctrines, the practical application of the rules of faith, and the customs that have become associated with these doctrines.

From south to north, from hills to plains, from conservatism to liberalism, from rejection of, to adaptation to American culture patterns, these are the main groups:

Old Order Amish or House Amish
Beachy Amish
Conservative Amish or Church Amish
Swiss Mennonites
Church of God in Christ
Old Mennonites
Old Order Wisler Mennonites
Mennonites
Middle District Conference, General Conference
New Amish, Apostolic Christian
Reformed Mennonites
Oak Grove Mennonites

The nomenclature can be only momentarily accurate, one must admit, because new alignments are constantly developing, and the researcher who tries to classify and bring order to the various groups is of necessity immediately outdated.

For instance, in the first group, the Old Order Amish, there exists the larger Swartzentruber and the small Stutzman and King offshoots, which differ about certain external minutiae such as the cut of hair, the size of the brim of the hat or the use of a glass window in the side of the buggy. Yet these items of differentiation are considered matters of salvation itself — and association with people who have not accepted them is forbidden.

The Old Order Amish distinguish themselves from the rest of the Mennonites by their definition of the "world," not by a difference in confessional doctrines. They cling tenaciously to a literal interpretation of the New Testament injunction of the separation of God's elect from the world.

The variance between the Old Order Amish and most Mennonite conferences lies in the interpretation and degree of application of the rule of separation. The Amish . . . interpret literally whatever doctrine and biblical passage they have once come to accept.

Rarely does an Amishman, as a single individual, venture forth alone into a locality not previously settled by Amish people. Several go together to found a colony.

In one instance, an individual family that had gone to a different section of the region returned within a very short time to the safe enclosure of the group. Again, three young families of one Amish district, who had dispersed into the outside "world" a few years before, safely retreated to the rural environment of their Amish district; they were welcomed and accepted as lost sheep come home.

Any member showing tendencies toward unaccustomed or irregular behavior is disciplined within the community. The rulers of the district keep a watchful eye over their flock. Non-conformists are warned in private, then brought to the attention of the "Gemei;"

if they still persist in the individualist behavior, they are expelled from the congregation.

On the other hand, the overseers give counsel and help to the needy. A widow with children is urged to remarry, and eligible men are suggested. Orphaned children are never sent to institutions and therefore, are no burden on the local welfare authority. Living on alms or on the fruits of somebody else's labor is not tolerated. Everybody, male and female, capable of giving physical assistance is required to do so.

The old people never sell out to retire to the city. Instead, they stay where they have always been. And if they cannot work any longer, their presence brings inspiration and comfort to younger members of the family. At the same time, each family provides for its sick and aged. If illness should cause an unmanageable hardship, then the district comes forward with aid.

To recognize an Amish home, one need only look for the presence of the horse and buggy, or if this should fail, a glance at the windows may tell the faith of the inhabitants.

Plain blue or green cloth curtains are the unmistakable characteristic of the Amish. Lace or ruffled curtains are taboo.

The "granddaddy house" is another characteristic of Amish settlements. Smaller than the family home, it is often its duplicate; at times it is a wing added, or

an extension built, to the side of the house. Amish grandparents vacate their home to a younger child. On the scene of their own greatest activity, the grandparents watch the family of one of their children grow, sharing still, in their own way, in the bustle of an active farm life.

The interior of the typical Amish home is very clean. The curtains of solid-colored blue or green cloth, the oilcloth on the table, the few, unmatched chairs, the odd cutlery, the plain chinaware or even tin or enameled plates, the iron bedstead in the most bare bedroom — all suggest the chaste frugality and restrained modesty of the Amish.

The absence of all pictures or portraits of present or past generations, of all other wall decorations, including wallpaper, of rugs or carpets, of knickknacks or art objects, of fancy quilts, covers or pillowcases heightens the impression of sobriety and austerity.

Television sets, radios, hi-fi combinations, phonographs and musical instruments are taboo.

No electric gadgets clutter up their kitchens. An odd table may hold a few religious books, including the big family Bible in German and perhaps the local newspaper. Magazines are notably absent. The Sugarcreek *Budget* brings weekly news from every other Amish district and from faraway settlements. In this plainness is a sense of order and pride.

Tradition demands that when an Amishman buys a

modern farm he remove all electric wiring, central heating and perhaps even running water. The kitchen tap, however, is generally favored over the old-fashioned hand pump and the heavy stone sink.

The two-story bank or Swiss barn is the marvel of the settlement. Under one roof, the Amish farmer concentrates all his indoor work and shelters all his animals, his grain, his feed and his implements. This economy of operation he has learned from long experience. After all, his farm is his wealth, the means of his livelihood.

The location and placing of the barn in relation to the house and the rest of the farm is considered. House and barn usually stand at right angles to each other, with a southern exposure preferable for the house. To create natural drainage, the barn usually stands on an incline in the contour of the landscape.

Amish beards are as familiar in Ohio as the buggy or the bonnet. When a man comes of marriageable age and has joined the church, he wears a beard. He also shaves his upper and lower lips, and, depending on the ruling of his particular congregation, he may shave his cheeks.

The bishop of an Amish district prescribes the length of the men's hair; it may be ordered to be as short as to the upper tips of the ear or as long as to a finger's width below the lobe of an ear.

Amishmen appear without their hats only inside a

house, school or at the Sunday meeting.

In the Amish community, women are more conservative than the men. The style of hat and the neckline of the hair of the men allow some variation; the women have no liberty in their coiffures. Their hair is parted in the middle, then brushed back and rolled, never braided, in a knot on the back of the head. Young girls do braid but do not allow the hair to hang from their heads. All the women wear identical white net prayer caps and black bonnets.

It is with the most conservative element within Amish society, solidly welded to its traditional behavior, that the ever-widening and penetrating American culture comes to wrestle.

There are inconsistencies, one observes, in the Amish adaptation to modern America. For instance, when they were taken to court over their boycott of a man for possessing an automobile, the defendants themselves hired a car to come to trial. They do not permit one of their own group to be a driver. And although they use tractors for belt-power to thresh and grind feed for their cattle, they, themselves, cannot use the tractor for plowing.

One wonders how it is possible that a distinctive group of people can stand aside here in the heart of modern America . . . and yet outwardly have no part of it. What gives them the strength to resist the seemingly irresistible conveniences — the automobile, the

tractor, electricity, refrigeration, radio, central heating?

It is not lack of mental alacrity . . . for these are shrewd and alert people.

Fundamental for all Mennonite bodies, including the Amish, is the content of the Schleitheim Confession of Faith of 1527 and the later Dortrecht Confession of Faith of 1632, both of which focus on these points:

Voluntary membership, with adult baptism as symbol of that membership; refusal to bear arms and to participate in government, whether local or national; communion and footwashing among members of the group; rejection of the oath; separation from nonbelievers; the expulsion of the unfaithful, but extensive mutual aid among all faithful members; the ordination of leaders of the local group.

The Amish place the focus of the argument of differentiation between themselves and every other group upon one word: "world." Every unadopted and unacceptable item of contemporary culture is decried as "worldly."

Editor's note: Information for this article was taken from the book "Our Amish Neighbors," published in 1962 and written by William I. Schreiber, a long-time German professor at The College of Wooster.

VARIOUS ORDERS LIVE IN HARMONY

By Rhonda Rosner

Differences in biblical applications set apart the different orders of the Amish. These differences, however, do not affect the Amish as a community, as neighbors or as friends, says Atlee D. Miller, a New Order Amishman who lives near Trail.

His neighborhood, he says, is composed of varying orders living in harmony.

Whether New Order or Old Order, all the Amish churches in Holmes County have descended from a remarkable Amishman who dressed in white.

Jonas "White" Stutzman (born 1788, died Oct. 18, 1871) was the first white man to settle in the Indian country of eastern Holmes County and the first Amish settler in the county.

Stutzman arrived in the spring of 1809 and settled south of Walnut Creek. He provided the county's

first sawmill and also served as a teacher.

About 1849, the settler became convinced that the world would end in 1853, and in booklet form, made three separate appeals "so that all men would be saved," Miller says. At the time of his prediction, "Der Weis" Stutzman donned white in preparation for the second coming of Christ.

In anticipation of his return, Stutzman built an oversized chair for the Lord. The chair, which was built without nails, has been kept in the Stutzman family over the years. Roman and Evelyn Stutzman — she is a direct descendant of the first settler — recently loaned the 145-year-old chair to the Mennonite Information Center near Berlin for display.

The founding father of the Holmes County Amish community was very conservative, Miller says. He and his wife and eight children later moved to the Martins Creek area. Stutzman requested that when he died he was not to be transported by vehicle. In honor of his wish, he was carried by his fellow church members the entire seven miles to his burial spot — a hillside family cemetery south of Walnut Creek.

The cemetery was razed in 1964 to provide fill dirt for a new road, and some remains and markers were relocated, according to the epitaph on Stutzman's tombstone. Stutzman's remains were reburied in the cemetery at the Walnut Creek Mennonite Church.

An Amish funeral procession

Many of the grave markers were lost in the transition, Miller says. Both Amish and non-Amish worked together to raise funds to purchase a new tombstone for Stutzman's grave. A fund was set up at local banks asking for donations for the marker. The stone gives a brief history of the first settler.

In Stutzman's time, Miller says, there were no "orders" of Amish. You were Amish or you weren't.

"A lot of the people around here are direct descendants of Jonas Stutzman," Miller says.

Today, there are seven orders of "horse-and-buggy" Amish in Holmes County, according to Miller.

Amish communities are divided into church districts, which number 140 in Holmes, Wayne, Tuscarawas and Stark counties and part of Coshocton County. Each district consists of 25 to 30 families. The New Order Amish, which are the most recently formed, comprise about 20 of the districts.

MURAL PORTRAYS HISTORY OF AMISH

By Amelia T. Reiheld

Visitors to Holmes County and the surrounding area often feel like Rip Van Winkle in reverse — as if they have awakened from a long nap to find themselves dumped a hundred years into the past.

They're curious about those horse-drawn buggies, the bearded men and bonneted women going about their everyday business dressed in old-fashioned garb and the farms worked by teams of sturdy draft horses.

Most tourists understand that the Mennonite and Amish heritage is much more than colorful quilts, fruit pies and picturesque farms, but nowhere is the culture's turbulent history more readily accessible than at the Mennonite Information Center, near Berlin. While the center's primary drawing card is "Behalt," visitors also find cordial volunteer staff

members who are willing to answer questions about the area's many attractions as well as about the Amish faith and its origins.

"Behalt," the word, means remember, or keep; "Behalt," the painting, is an enormous circular mural that's 10-feet high and 265-feet long. It provides a dramatic pictorial history of Holmes County's most visible residents.

The centerpiece of the Mennonite Information Center, this "cyclorama" depicts the journey in faith of the Anabaptists and their modern-day descendants — the Mennonites, the Hutterites and the Amish from the time of Christ's resurrection through the Reformation and subsequent persecution, to the present day.

Some 30 years in the planning and nearly 14 years in its execution, with a somewhat stormy history of its own, the painting was first opened for exhibit in mid-1990. Artist Heinz Gaugel finally completed and signed his opus magnum in October of 1992.

Since then, thousands of visitors from all over the world have flocked individually and by the busload to the Mennonite Information Center to learn more of their own background or to better understand the people of Holmes County.

The cyclorama is full of drama, tragedy, hope and inexorable moving onward. Sweeping swaths of background color provide transition from one period to another, as well as emphasizing the changing moods within the painting. Violent reds, oranges and purples clash throughout the scenes of European persecution of the Anabaptists by established churches, both Roman Catholic and Protestant. There's an interplay of predominating golds and greens as Mennonite and Amish come to the fertile New World and set about creating a place for themselves where they might practice their religious beliefs unhindered.

German immigrant and self-taught artist Gaugel was incredulous when he first stumbled upon the anachronistic Ohio communities.

"At first, he didn't believe what we told him about our history," says Verna Schlabach, the director of the center. "He did research of his own off and on for about 30 years," she explains, saying that the artist combed libraries and church records both in this country and in Europe for information and decided there was a story that had to be told. He set about finding sponsors for his proposed work, which he underestimated would take two years to complete.

"Behalt" is said to be the only cyclorama in the United States entirely researched and executed by one person. Although other artists occasionally joined Gaugel on the scaffolding, he found it so difficult to explain what he wanted done that it was easier to do it all himself. Actual paint-brush wielding time amounted to nearly four years.

"Behalt" creator Heinz Gaugel

Gaugel, himself, is not aligned with any religious denomination, but felt a kinship with the Mennonite and Amish doctrine of nonviolence. His other artwork, including a number of mosaics and murals, has characteristically been on a large scale, and increasingly dealt with religious themes, although "Behalt" is described as a historical treatment rather than a theological one.

"When you see the thing, you begin to make sense of our history," Schlabach says. The painting's scope and complexity make it something many visitors will want to see again. "I was here most of a year before I began to feel as if I had really seen it all."

In addition to the epic painting, the visitor's center offers a 20-minute slide program explaining the customs, beliefs and lifestyles of today's Amish and Mennonites. A gift shop features crafts from the Mennonite Central Committee's self-help projects around the world, as well as local products.

Section III
Customs
& Traditions

BUGGIES ARE PLAIN, PRACTICAL

By Amelia T. Reiheld

"It comes in any color you want, so long as it's black."

Surprisingly enough, there's still personal transportation manufactured to Henry Ford's most famous specification.

While an Ohio Amishman can order his buggy with seating for two, or six or more, with a windshield or without, for hauling a large family to Sunday services or pigs to auction, with one "horsepower" or more rarely, two, he can be sure of one thing — that buggy will be black.

An Amish buggy is plain, practical and always appropriate, especially convenient features for a vehicle built to last a lifetime. After 10 or 15 years, the wheels may need to be replaced, or the interior recovered, but the basic works of a buggy — the wooden

framework, the axles and the steel springs — are nearly indestructible. Furthermore, a horse and buggy serves as an all-weather vehicle that will roll right through snow too deep for automobiles.

There are nearly 30 buggy manufacturers in Wayne and Holmes counties. Each is capable of producing some three dozen custom-made, hand-built buggies each year, most of which stay right in the immediate area. Some buggies, however, are shipped all over the United States. The wait, from the time an order is placed to the time the buggy is delivered, can be as long as a year-and-a-half at some of the more popular shops.

To the untrained eye the buggies look as alike as peas in a pod, but each one has been built to its owner's specifications, which depend in part, on the rules and customs of his church district. For Old Order Amish, the buggy will have steel-rimmed wheels and the side curtains will roll up. New Order Amish may have rubber rims on their tires for a quieter, more comfortable ride, and sliding doors. The very conservative Swartzentruber Amish won't be ordering the Plexiglas windshield, the reflective tape on the back or even headlights and tail lights, opting instead for a single kerosene lantern on the side.

There's a fancy, scalloped sunscreen across the front, just beneath the top of the buggy that's popular with young people, but their elders seem to prefer

something a little plainer. Other options to be considered when ordering a new buggy include a hand-operated windshield wiper, brakes, headlights of shiny chrome and even a dome light inside.

Although the newest buggies are quite comfortable and weather resistant, with propane heaters and storm screens, many older folk keep warm on bitter days with lap blankets and gallon plastic milk jugs filled with hot water.

One genial Amish used-buggy salesman insists that all his vehicles come with air-conditioning as standard equipment, as he demonstrates the roll-up curtains on sides and rear. The salesman points to a key dangling from a switch in the center of the buggy's dash. "Know what that's for? To start the engine, of course." A tourist, solemnly listening to the man's colorful spiel, looks momentarily puzzled, then asks how to operate the battery-powered headlights.

While black is the only color available for the outside of Amish buggies, the interior can be any one of a rainbow of shades. Upholstery material is usually a crushed velvet, often a rich royal blue or emerald green, although choices range in fanciness from the simplest black leatherette to a deep pile plush. Little rumble seats can be built into the back of the standard buggy, just right for the small children who can often be seen peeking out through the back, waving shyly to motorists.

Most buggy shops order the wooden wheels, the axles, bearings and steel springs from other suppliers. The framework of the buggy itself, the upholstery and the shafts to which the horse is harnessed are generally produced in the carriage-maker's shop. The framing is mostly of poplar, ash, masonite and plywood, and the wheels are made from hickory. All the exterior woodwork is painted with numerous coats of black enamel and buffed to a high gloss.

While a buggy shop doesn't quite operate like Henry Ford's assembly line, in a typical operation, there are often two or three buggies in several stages of completion. There may be a couple being framed in one part of the shop, while the paint is drying on several others. In yet another area, the carriage-maker's wife or sister staples upholstery fabric to a nearly completed buggy and sews seat cushions.

By one buggy builder's estimate, there are 100 man-hours in the building of a good carriage, and his family-run shop figures to roll out three a month. His customers know they'll have to put their order in at least nine months ahead of time.

Amish carriage-makers generally will use pneumatic tools such as paint sprayers and staplers that are driven by a diesel-powered air compressor, but most of the shops have no electrical power. The workers build by the light of kerosene lamps on cloudy days. As one buggy-maker explained it, "the compressed

Page 58

air is good for powering the tools — and that's all. If you open the door to electric tools, though, it's hard to draw the line there, and pretty soon, you have television and all the rest."

An Amish boy will begin to harness a horse himself and drive buggies short distances as soon as he is tall enough to do the job, perhaps 10 years old. He will likely be given his first buggy, a used one, when he's 14 or 15, just out of school. He will be working as a hired hand, often on nearby farms, and bringing his paycheck home to his parents for the next five years or more. When he's about 21, or when he gets married, his parents will buy him a brand new buggy, an investment of nearly $2,000, or up to $2,500 for the deluxe model — horse and harness not included.

Boys being boys, it's not entirely unheard of for teenagers to hold late-night buggy races on back country roads. The buggy horses are often ones that didn't quite make the grade on the harness racing circuit, but are still pretty spirited animals. Although such goings-on are unsanctioned by Amish parents, it's a natural temptation for a young man with a frisky horse and a fine lightweight buggy to see what she'll do — especially when challenged.

According to one buggy-maker, there's surprisingly little damage to vehicle or driver from the rare accidental encounter between two buggies. Accidents between buggies and cars or trucks, of course, are an-

other story.

While Amish girls learn early to harness the horses and drive buggies, they don't generally own their own buggies unless they've remained unmarried. Young women receive trousseaus of dishes, linens and furniture instead.

By the time an Amish family is established on a farm, its shed will hold an assortment of carts, hacks and buggies, and perhaps even a sleigh. Each vehicle is meant for a specific purpose. The newest buggy, usually a single-seater, is kept polished to an immaculate shine, and is used for special occasions, such as weddings and funerals, and for transporting the family to church services, which are held every other week at the home of one of the families in the district.

There may be several buggies for everyday use, depending on how many children in the family are old enough to drive. A large family might own a two-seat buggy, which is the Amish version of the station wagon. Naturally, no self-respecting young man would dream of borrowing the stodgy two-seater to take to the Sunday evening social.

Farmers often use the horse-drawn equivalent of a pickup truck, called a hack, which has a long narrow bed, good for taking bales of hay or a hog to market, or bringing home enough groceries for a very large family. A hack may be an open wagon, with cargo space behind the driver's seat, or it may be a "top-

hack," with an enclosed cab to shield its occupants from bad weather.

Horse-drawn carriages, aside from being practical, durable and dependable, are central to the Amish way of life. In their efforts to avoid worldliness, Amish folk strive to keep their families close to home and centered around an agricultural lifestyle.

While they will accept rides with non-Amish people or hire drivers to take them for a distance, owning cars is, as one Amish woman puts it, "too easy." The temptation to just hop in the car and go to town, or

Here's an "inside" view of what an Amish buggy driver sees.

across the country, leads to a fragmentation of the society and exposes them to a world that is too fast and glitzy to be compatible with the plain way of life.

Few buggy-makers seem to have much idea of the history behind their craft. An elderly Amishman, when asked why buggies developed to their present style, shrugs his shoulders and justifies the tradition with a phrase that explains so many things Amish: "It's just our way."

These wheels are ready to go on new buggies.

An Account of a Buggy Ride

By John Roepke

This marks my third month as a resident of Holmes County. In that time, I have traveled all over the county. I have been to most of the bigger villages and have sat in all the important meetings with all the important officials.

But the only thing people seem to ask me about, especially if I go home to Lakewood (Ohio) on the weekends, is what are the Amish and Mennonites like? It is a curious question to me, because many of the people I know only know Holmes County for having a large Amish and Mennonite population.

My friends and family seem to have this odd fascination with them simply because their lifestyle is so different from theirs and mine. I can say I was guilty of this, too, but now that I live and work amongst them, I am getting used to them as people, not some

curious culture.

Slowly, I am learning a lot more about them. One way I am doing this is through a friend who is Amish. My friend doesn't want to be in the paper, so I will respect the request and not print that person's name. I can say the person is very nice and friendly.

Since I've been here, the one thing I was curious about was what it was like to ride in a real Amish buggy. I know I could get a horse and carriage ride, but that would seem too touristy for me.

That is where my friend comes in. That person offered to give me a ride. Of course I jumped at the chance. Let me tell you, it was worth it.

Despite the rather loud squeaking of the buggy and the "clippity-clop" from the horse, my host and I had a surprisingly pleasant conversation in which I learned a few things about the Amish culture that I didn't know before.

One of them was that the Amish have church services at a person's home, and they transport the benches for the services in a "bench wagon."

I say this because we passed the bench wagon as it was going to a home for that week's services. The wagon was being pulled by a tractor, and the funny noise it made had the horse a little frightened. Me, too, I have to admit, until it came around the corner and we were finally able to see what it was.

The buggy was an open-air model and a little

dusty. My host apologized for its dirty appearance. To me it was just perfect, seeing as how a little dirt never bothered me. I did like feeling the wind in my hair.

Riding along in the open air was much like driving a convertible. We were lucky because the weather was cool that day; the bugs stayed away. The quilt we used to keep our legs warm more than did the job.

After the ride, my host gave me a tour of the house. For the sake of my host's privacy, all I can say is that it is a very beautiful house, with wide spaces for socializing and working. There is no TV, radio or any electrical appliance to be found.

My host's sister was making loaves of bread and was kind enough to offer me one. I accepted (I'm not stupid) and enjoyed it very much.

That is the one thing that has struck me about all the Amish I've encountered. They are extraordinarily kind — from the workers at places I've shopped and done stories, to people shopping at stores or flea markets. They go out of their way to help you. It is a nice feeling when that happens. They are quick with an answer, which is usually correct and thoughtful.

But most of all, except for their cultural beliefs being different from the "English," as they call us, they are similar to every person I've ever met.

They laugh and cry, smile, hug, run, jump and yell. There seems to be no difference. They are protective

of their kids and the whole family. They buy stuff, sell stuff and trade stuff. Just like everybody.

They follow the word of their God seriously. That is the main guiding influence on their lives, and there is nothing wrong or odd about that.

The best thing I can say about the Amish is they just want the respect and courtesy of the people around them. It turns out to be a good thing that my dad, long ago, taught me the Golden Rule and to respect everybody for their beliefs.

CLOTHING SETS THEM APART

By Janet Williard

To the casual observer, the one thing that visually sets the Amish apart the most from the rest of the world is their style of dress. Their unique clothing style symbolizes submission to the church and binds the Amish together as a social group.

Clothing worn by the Amish communicates information about the individual wearer, the occasion and group ties. The mode of dress is organized around three social occasions — work, dress-up and church.

Because each group of Amish is slightly different, it is difficult for outsiders to distinguish group membership by the varied clothing styles. But the Amish easily recognize each other by their clothing styles.

Ada K. Yoder, a member of the Holmesville Northwest Church District, says that dress rules are set by church councils. The rules are unwritten for the Old Order Amish, but are known by all members.

Yoder provided the information for this "primer" about the Amish style of dress:

Women's Clothing

The head coverings that Amish women wear are made of organdy or silk-like fabric. They have multiple pleats and a tiny bow — about two inches long by a fourth-inch wide at the back.

For girls, the everyday color may be white or black, but black is always worn for church. After marriage, only white may be worn.

The ribbon ties are sometimes uncut for everyday wear, but are always cut for church wear.

The covering symbolizes subjection to God and to man, and Amish women cover their heads at all times.

Women's dresses are made in a one-piece style, with a pleated skirt. Young girls' dresses button at the back, while adult women use snap fasteners or straight pins. The length of the skirts and sleeves vary, as do the necklines and the fullness of sleeves.

Women's dresses for church or dress-up occasions are made with dark fabric — blue, gray, wine, purple or green. Black is always worn for communion and funerals. Everyday dresses are made of lighter colors — mint green, peach, light blue or lavender.

Amish girls and women usually wear some type of garment over their dresses. The cape is triangular and pinned at the waistline in the back. The sides are then brought over the shoulders and fastened with pins at the front. Girls up to age 15 wear the cape ends crossed at the front; after age 15, the ends are worn straight.

The apron also is attached with pins. For church services, a white cape and apron are worn. For dress-up occasions, a wedding for instance, the cape and apron match the color of the dress. The Swartzentruber Amish always wear a contrasting color of cape and apron, however. For everyday wear, a tie-on apron may be worn.

Young girls sometimes wear a pinafore-like apron.

Black stockings and black tie shoes usually are worn by women of all ages. Stockings are made of cotton and occasionally nylon. In recent years, adults as well as children and youths, have begun to wear sneakers or "tennis shoes" for casual wear, Yoder says.

A black shawl and bonnet complete a woman's wardrobe. Girls often wear a homemade coat for school. The bonnet is worn over the covering. The shawl is fastened with pins. In the winter, a head scarf is sometimes worn, along with gloves and rubber boots.

Persons of the Amish faith may not wear jewelry of

An Amish family enjoys some cotton candy.

any kind. Watches and wedding bands are strictly forbidden by the church.

In Holmes County, a wide choice of fabrics are permitted, as long as they are not too "fancy." However, in other areas of Ohio, fabrics such as knits are forbidden. Clothing is always made of solid-color fabrics.

All Amish clothing is made at home on a treadle sewing machine. Each woman usually makes most of the family's clothing, but for difficult items, like a mutza coat, she may have a relative or friend who is a more skilled seamstress sew the garment.

Men's Clothing

A broad-brimmed hat symbolizes the Amish man.

Black felt hats are worn in the winter and straw hats are worn in the warm months. The width of the brim and hat band, and the height and shape of the crown vary. Old Order Amish wear hats with a three-inch brim, while the Swartzentruber Amish wear hats with a four-inch brim. Boys sometimes wear dark-colored knit hats in the winter.

A man's hair is generally cut in a "bowl style." It is cut evenly all the way around the head, or in a "notched" cut in which the bangs are cut shorter than the hair at the temples. The hair is always combed forward from the crown and never is parted. Men begin growing a beard following baptism, but they do not wear mustaches.

"Broadfall" trousers without hip pockets or zippers are made for the men. A flap runs across the entire front of the trousers and fastens with four buttons. The trousers are loose-fitting and are usually kept in place with suspenders, which may be made of the same fabric as the trousers, or may be purchased. Depending on the church group, the suspenders may make an "X," "H" or "Y" shape at the back.

For church, men wear black, dark gray or dark blue

suits. A church coat, called a "mutza," or a plain-cut jacket is always worn in the winter, but may be omitted in the summer. A vest is always worn for church. Shirts may be of the three-button pullover style with a standing collar, or they may be coat style with a turnover collar. Boys wear dark pants and white shirts for church. Everyday shirts may be light in color.

    High-laced shoes — black for church and brown or tan for work — are the most common footwear for men, although low-cut shoes are sometimes worn. Youngsters favor tennis shoes. Rubber boots are worn over the shoes for barn work or in bad weather.

AMISH QUILTS ARE WORKS OF ART

By Janet Williard

The hand-stitched quilt. Contemporary, yet timeless. A work of art with a utilitarian function.

Generations of Amish women have perfected the technique that turns plain fabric into a thing of beauty. Learning to quilt and sew is literally child's play for Amish girls. They use scrap fabric to pretend to sew. Sometimes they sew buttons onto the fabric.

"It's something we grow up with," says Rebecca Beachy of Sugarcreek. "When I was a young girl, my mom used to quilt and I watched her — how she did it, how she put her needle in."

The children learn the art of quilting and sewing not only from their mothers, but from other women as well. Amish women seldom use baby-sitters. When families or church groups gather to sew or quilt, the children go along and watch what the

Some Amish-made quilts on display

women are doing.

Martha Miller of Walnut Creek describes how her oldest daughter began quilting: "I gave her some old scrap material and put it in a small frame. I traced around (a design), I think it was a bird, and she tried to quilt that. I put it away for her, for a keepsake of her first quilting."

Beachy says her daughter, who was 13 or 14 years old at the time, began quilting on an actual quilt.

"I put a quilt in (the frame) one day, and I said she should learn to quilt, and she got her thimble and her scissors, and sat down.

"The first time you quilt," Beachy says, "you usually have to take it (the stitches) out. She'll (my daughter) quilt, and then she'll take it out, and then she'll do it again. You just have to watch and see that your stitches aren't too big."

Beachy's daughter's first quilt "was one that was for her own bed, actually. Now, if it had been a quilt I was going to sell or put in an auction or something, I wouldn't have let her help."

Sometimes, a girl's first project will be a pillow top that can be placed in a small frame and held on her lap as she quilts.

Selecting a pattern is the first step in quilt-making. A variety of patterns is available at quilt shops — from the traditional to the contemporary.

Next, the fabric is selected. Then, it is cut out according to the pattern. In the next step, called piecing, the units of the pattern are sewn together into a quilt top. A simple pattern can be pieced in a day, but one that is unfamiliar may take a week.

The quilt top usually is pieced by machine. Then the backing, the batting, and the quilt top are layered, put in a frame and quilted.

A variety of quilting designs are used, some smaller and more intricate than others. Patterns and templates for the quilting design also are available in quilt shops. The design is marked on the fabric, using a special quilting pencil that washes out. The women mark the quilt as faintly as possible, so it's just visible during the quilting.

Sometimes, the quilts used in Amish homes are plain, solid-colored fabric. The only "decoration" is the quilted design itself.

Amish women often quilt as a group project, but they quilt individually, too. A quilting frame can be set up at home.

Amish girls learn to sew both by hand and by machine. Some sewing machines operate by using a treadle. Others use a battery. Some even use a solar-powered battery. The choice varies by church district.

Whatever the method, sewing is a necessity for the Amish women. Almost all clothing is made at home. After all, there is no place to buy ready-made, Amish-style clothing.

LATE FALL IS THE TIME FOR WEDDINGS

By Rhonda Rosner

Blue may not be the most traditional color for a bride's gown, but in the case of the Amish, it is the most popular choice.

Blue is the typical color chosen for weddings by young Amish women. Navy blue and sky blue are the most popular colors of Amish brides in any year.

An Amish bride's wedding attire is always new. She usually makes her own dress, and the attendants — known as "newehockers" or "sidesitters" — make their own dresses from material that is provided by the bride-to-be.

The style of the dresses is plain cut and mid-calf in length. They are unadorned; there is no fancy trim or lace, and there is never a train. The bride and her attendants also wear capes and aprons over their dresses. Instead of a veil, the bride wears a black prayer covering to differentiate from the white cap she wears daily.

All members of an Old Order Amish wedding party wear dark stockings and black Sunday shoes with ties. No one carries flowers.

Most non-Amish brides wear their bridal dresses once, but an Amish bride's practical dress will serve her for more than just her wedding day, as it will become her Sunday church attire after she is married.

The groom and his newehockers wear suits of dark blue, dark gray, navy or black. All coats and vests fasten with hooks and eyes, not buttons. Their shirts are white.

Pennsylvania Amish will sometimes don bow ties for the wedding, but in this area, the men do not. They wear black hats with a three-inch brim.

All of the attendants in the wedding party play a vital role in the events of the day. There is no best man or maid-of-honor; all are of equal importance.

The Amish normally favor November and part of December as wedding dates. This is when the harvest has been completed and severe winter weather has not yet arrived. But weddings are held throughout the year, though usually not in July.

The wedding is preceded by several weeks of preparation. Extensive cleaning takes place during the last week. Dinnerware, silverware, kettles, potato mashers, knives, frying pans and even stoves are bor-

rowed as needed from friends and neighbors.

The engagement is supposed to be a secret until it is announced or "published" on a Sunday. The event takes place about a week-and-a-half later, often on the second Thursday afterward, but it can be as much as a month later. The most common days for a wedding are Tuesday and Thursday for Old Order Amish. Members of the newer orders sometimes marry on Saturday.

In this area, the bride's mother is usually the chief organizer of the work before the wedding and of the events on ceremony day. She is assisted by relatives, neighbors and by friends from the bride's church district. Since the wedding dinner is not catered, friends and family members serve as cooks and waiters.

A typical Amish wedding day begins at 4 a.m., or even earlier. After all, the cows must still be milked and all the other daily farm chores need to be done. Helpers begin frying chickens by 5 a.m.

Twenty or more cooks and 20 waiters prepare and serve the meal. Cooks are the couple's mothers, sisters and sisters-in-law, aunts and sometimes even grandmothers. The groom's mother usually prepares the meat.

By 7 a.m., the people in the wedding party have eaten breakfast, changed into their wedding clothes and are waiting to greet the guests.

Typically, some 200 to 400 relatives, friends and

Hand-crafted signs decorate a wedding party's carriage.

church members are invited to the ceremony, which is held in the bride's home or at a neighbor's. Serving as usher is the bride's father or the man of the house where the wedding is held.

Dinner- and silverware already have been set on the tables before the day of the ceremony, sometimes as long as a week in advance.

Many times, an Amish family will be invited to several weddings in the same day. Therefore, some guests come for part of the day-long affair. Some come in the morning for the ceremony, others for the noon meal and still others for supper in the evening.

The "forgehers," or ushers (usually four married

couples), will make sure each guest has a place on one of the long wooden benches in the meeting or church room of the home. At 8:30 a.m., the three-hour-long service begins. The congregation will sing hymns — without instrumental accompaniment — while the minister counsels the bride and groom in another part of the house.

After the minister and the young couple return to the church room, a prayer, scripture reading and sermon take place. Typically, the sermon is long. The minister discusses marriage stories throughout the Old and New testaments. The minister finishes by reading Tobias, a book about marriage in the Apocrypha, a collection of books that was part of the original Bible but was deleted from current editions.

After the sermon is concluded, the minister asks the bride and groom to step forward from the rest of the congregation. Then, he questions them about their marriage, which is similar to taking wedding vows.

The minister then blesses the couple. After the blessing, other ordained men and the fathers of the couple may give testimony about marriage. A final prayer draws the ceremony to a close.

That's when the festivities begin and the women get ready to serve dinner.

The tables are set up in a U-shape around the walls of the living room, with a corner of the center table

reserved for the bride and groom and the bridal party. This is an honored place called the "Eck," meaning corner.

The bride sits on the groom's left. The groom's witnesses sit beside him, and the bride's witnesses beside her, with the women to the left.

A separate table is set for all the ministers, bishops and deacons.

A Young Couple Talks About Life

By Kevin Lynch

The prospect of starting a new life together as husband and wife can be an intimidating time for any young couple.

Along with facing the challenge of leaving the nest and starting a nest of their own, young couples face a world of differences as they begin life together.

This time is no different for an Amish couple. Despite a different culture, they face many of the same fears and first-year ups and downs as any other couple.

Glen and Ina Mast of Trail were married on Oct. 6, 1994, and their first year of marriage has been fun and eventful, they say.

Glen, 24, works at Wayne-Dalton in Mount Hope. There are many ways in which his life has changed since tying the knot last year, he says.

A young couple and child — complete with a balloon — take a Sunday ride.

"What I really like about being married is coming home and having a wife here to greet me. I like being married.

"One of the biggest changes for me is not being able to go anywhere whenever I feel like it. I've got to start thinking that it's not just for myself anymore."

He admits that whenever a horse sale or something like that comes up — something he used to just go to whenever he wanted — he now has to make sure it won't interfere with something he and Ina have planned.

Ina Mast, 19, works at the Amish Door Furniture store in Wilmot. But she will give up her job to become a mother when the time comes. She says it is not uncommon for Amish wives to work prior to becoming a parent.

"The double income is very helpful right now," Glen Mast says. "It's giving us an opportunity to buy our first home. We'll be moving into a house in the next few months over by my in-laws."

"I like working because I don't think I could just sit around the house all day. I'd probably get bored without a job," Ina Mast admits, although recently her workload has been very heavy. She has been working six days a week because of personnel changes at work.

Married life is keeping the couple busy as the Masts prepare for their first home.

"Keeping things in order around the house is probably the toughest part about being married," Ina Mast says. "I used to depend on mom a lot to do that. It's going to be nice moving back close to the family again.

"We see them basically every week, but I was used to being around them a lot more than that. That's been quite a change."

The Masts said they didn't have any special plans for their first anniversary. "We might go out to dinner," Glen Mast said.

BIRTHING CENTER SERVES AMISH WELL

By Amelia T. Reiheld

Babies were born at home, and Aunt Sadie, the neighborhood midwife, or ol' Doc, if somebody could find him in time, would attend to the technicalities of welcoming the newest member of the family.

As the demands on the doctors' time became more pressing and as medical science produced high-tech solutions to obstetrical emergencies, hospitals took over for Aunt Sadie. Having babies at home seems like a nice old-fashioned concept, but it just isn't done anymore, not even in the heart of Ohio's Amish country, where many other trappings of the 20th century world are rejected.

The Amish are as aware as everyone else that in a home birth there are just too many things that might go wrong for both mother and child that can be prevented with the help of modern medicine. And doc-

tors are simply kept too busy to be able to attend home births.

Still, there are many area women who don't want to go all the way to the city to have their babies. For many years Barb Hostetler, an Amish midwife, delivered babies at her home near Fredericksburg, often with the help of area physicians. But by the mid-1970s, she was ready to begin slowing down. Dr. Elton Lehman, a Mount Eaton osteopathic physician who had worked with her for years, proposed building the Mount Eaton Care Center, at which Hostetler would continue to work.

With funds raised entirely by contributions from the Mennonite and Amish communities, the Mount Eaton Care Center opened its doors in November 1985, with Lehman as its director. Since then, more than 2,500 babies have been born there.

Perched atop the second highest hill in Ohio, the birthing center, an attractive two-story brick building, boasts a fine view over village, fields of corn shocks and pastures.

It's an idyllic setting, to be sure, but having a baby at the Mount Eaton Care Center isn't for everybody. If you're likely to have complications or to need surgery, it's not for you. If you expect someone else to care for, bathe and change your baby, and take it away for the night, it's not for you. If you want to have nurses and aides waiting on you hand and foot, and have meals appear as if by magic, it's not for you.

In fact, if you're not Amish or conservative Mennonite, it's not for you.

The birthing center is a private institution with its services limited to members of those churches and others who live nearby. There are no surgical facilities, and consequently, the potential patients are carefully screened to minimize the chance of obstetrical emergencies. Patients with diabetes or high blood pressure, who are expecting multiple births or whose babies aren't properly positioned head-down will deliver at a hospital.

Even the weather plays a part in the decision. One Amish family was all set to deliver at the birthing center, but when the time came, there was a major snow storm in progress. Lehman says he told the expectant mother that if anything went wrong, there was no way they'd be able to make a safe emergency transfer to the hospital from Mount Eaton. The doctor bundled his patient into his Jeep, and followed a snow plow to a Massillon hospital, where, of course, everything went fine.

The clinic doesn't carry malpractice insurance, a situation that suits its Amish clientele just fine. Lehman recalls a recent phone call from a Cleveland woman who wanted to arrange for her delivery at Mount Eaton. Lehman told the woman he'd be happy

to talk with her, but he doubted that she qualified for admission. The woman became very angry and assured the doctor that he would hear from her lawyer. He did, too. It's a graphic illustration of precisely why the admission criteria are the way they are.

"In the Amish or Mennonite communities, if someone wanted to bring suit, the church would get after them, and pressure them to drop the case," Lehman says.

The interior decor is one of functional but pleasant simplicity. A small waiting room doubles as an area where meals may be prepared and heated. Due to state regulations, there is no kitchen, and meals are the responsibility of the patient and her family. Many bring their own food; some send out to the little restaurant down the road.

Patients and their families also are welcome to purchase the snacks and frozen dinners that are stored in the little waiting room. Each room has a small refrigerator, and patients may use the microwave ovens.

Each of the eight spacious patient rooms has its own bathroom. The rooms are usually private, but in a busy spell, two compatible mothers and their infants may share a room after delivery. A ninth room, sometimes used for large family visits, also can be pressed into service if necessary. The record census is 13 mothers and their babies in the center at once, with four rooms doubled up.

Labor, delivery and recovery all take place in the same room. Almost all the furniture was custom-made by local craftsmen to Dr. Lehman's specifications — even the delivery table, which is wheeled into the patient's room when it's needed. The bassinets, too, are more like furniture than hospital equipment. Clear panels are trimmed with oak spindles for the baby's bed. Beneath there's an oak-paneled cabinet for storing spare diapers and receiving blankets.

Two of the rooms are painted a traditional light blue color, and are equipped with kerosene wall lamps in an effort to make the very strict Swartzentruber Amish patients feel at home. Lehman says the lamps rarely are used, though, even by the most conservative families.

Because of state regulations for staffing, there's no separate nursery as such. Each baby rooms with its mother during the entire stay. Of course, the nurse's station boasts rocking chairs and space for bassinets for times when new mothers need a break or if a baby's bilirubin level is too high and it needs to spend some time under the special lights.

While Lehman and his Mount Eaton colleague, Dr. Nolan Byler, deliver most of the babies born at the care center, there are half a dozen other area physi-

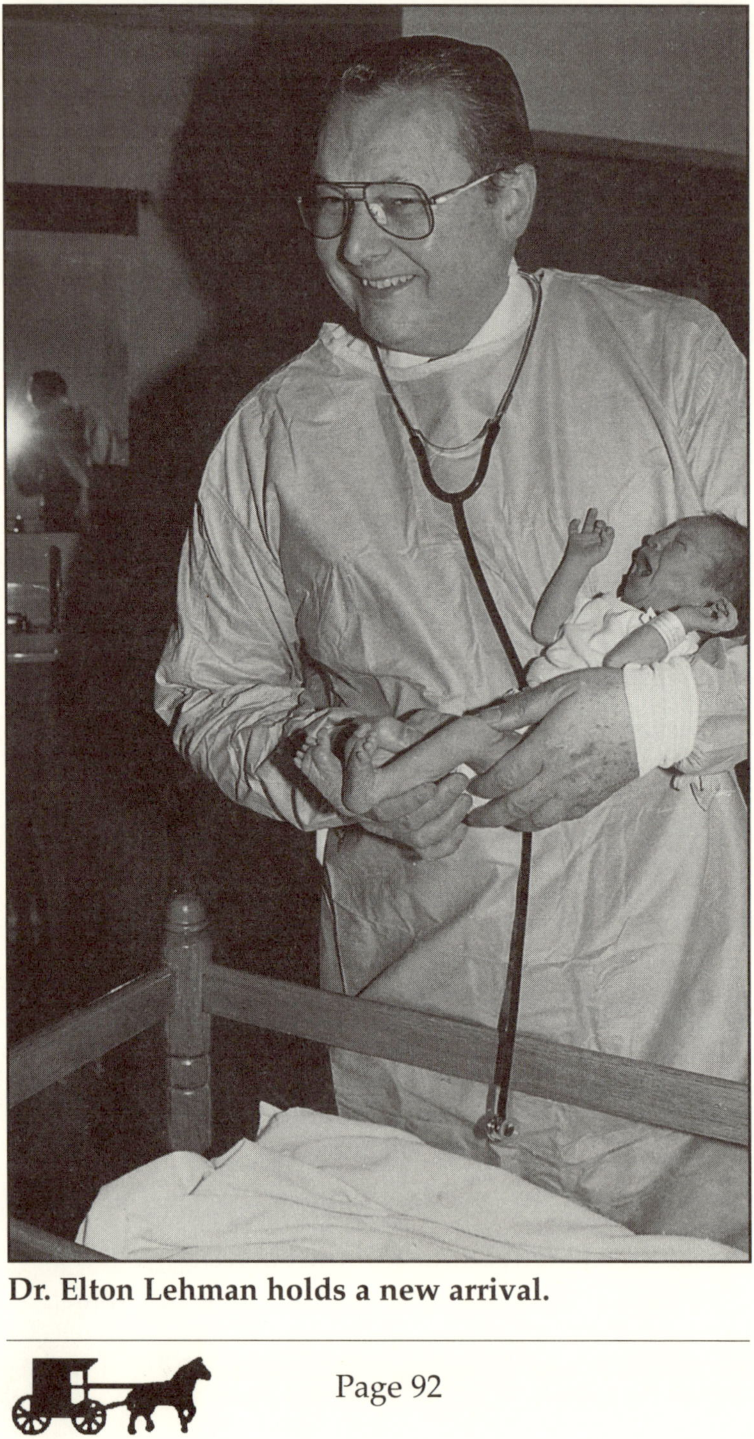

Dr. Elton Lehman holds a new arrival.

cians who attend obstetrical patients there, too. Each doctor is responsible for bringing his own equipment and providing a nurse to assist him during deliveries. The center's staff nurse also is there to help.

A single price, cash on the barrel-head, includes a 72-hour stay, with most patients staying at least two days after they deliver.

The Amish women approach obstetrics somewhat differently than the rest of his general practice, Lehman says. For one thing, Amish women tend to be more stoic and matter-of-fact. There's much more family support, and they rely more heavily on advice from their parents. The most striking difference, Lehman says, is that "every Amish baby is very much wanted and loved. It's always a very happy occasion."

Predictably, Lehman has some stories.

"Before we had the good emergency squad in Mount Eaton," he says, "I used to take Amish patients to the hospital in Massillon in the back seat of my own car."

He was stopped at a traffic light on the outskirts of town, he recalls, and a voice from the back seat said, "The baby's coming."

Lehman turned around to check on his patient, and, sure enough, the little one wasn't going to wait.

"I delivered the baby, and was ready to go when the light turned green."

Lehman says the car behind him was completely unaware of the drama.

When couples press Lehman for a prediction about the sex of their baby, the doctor hazards a guess — and then writes down the other option in his records. When he told them correctly, they remember it, and are impressed with his accuracy.

But when other parents kid him about guessing wrong, he points to his charted prediction. "See here? It's right here in black and white."

It's hard to argue with that. Besides, with the excitement of a brand new baby in the family, nobody's in a mood to quibble over details.

Friends, Church Provide Insurance

By Amelia T. Reiheld

"Sunny" Keim, a 41-year-old Amishman, just underwent open-heart surgery a couple of weeks ago. By the time the Apple Creek man is back on his feet, he will have accumulated perhaps $40,000 in medical bills. Like other members of the Old Order faith, though, he has no health insurance.

According to Old Order Amish deacon Eli A. S. Miller, also of Apple Creek, most Amish folk believe that scripture bans insurance. Life and health are gifts from God, and to purchase insurance is a form of gambling with those gifts. Using that argument, the Amish have successfully resisted paying the Social Security tax, in part because it's another form of insurance.

The Amish people have always looked after their own, traditionally accepting neither public charity

nor government aid. Perhaps part of the cement that holds the communities together is their mutual interdependence.

Everyone is expected to work and to contribute to his society for as long as he is able, but those who, because of old age or infirmity, are unable to do so, will be cared for by their family and fellow church members. The church members give alms before communion, which occurs twice a year. This offering then goes to support those of the community who are in need.

"But something had to be done about medical costs," Miller says. "If something happened, well, there's the farm . . ."

With an expansive wave of his arm toward his barn, his livestock and his fields, he indicates how easily doctor and hospital bills for a serious accident, major surgery or chronic illness could wipe out his life's work.

That could have been the case for Sunny Keim, who now has two very expensive new heart valves. Fortunately, he and many other area members of his faith banded together three years ago to establish a fund to cover catastrophic medical expenses. The members of a hundred Old Order Amish church districts in Wayne, Holmes, Knox, and Coshocton counties contribute the equivalent of one day's wages for each worker in the family into the church fund every

six weeks or so.

The deacon in every member church district collects the appropriate contribution from his 20 or 30 families, and sends it to the treasurer for the fund. Each member family is responsible for the first $2,000 of the year's medical bills, and a fourth of the next $20,000. The church fund covers the rest.

One major difference between the Amish fund and the insurance that "English" folk purchase is that "this is non-profit. Nobody gets rich off it this way," Miller explains. "So far, we're doing all right, but sometimes the money will run a little low."

When that happens, he says, the congregations hold fund-raisers, selling coupons for pizzas in cooperation with a local pizza parlor, or holding quilt sales.

Another approach to paying doctor bills that the Amish use from time to time is the age-old system of barter. Miller recalls a tragic accident in which five Amish children were killed. Several other children were taken to Cleveland and Akron hospitals, and the medical bills were astronomical.

"I called the doctors," Miller says, "and asked them if they'd give us a discount for paying cash. Most of them said, 'Sure,' but one doctor said, 'I'd rather just have a handmade quilt and call it even.'"

The three families got together and made a quilt for the physician, who wrote off his entire $1,500 bill.

Not all Amish church districts participate in the fund. The most conservative sects, including the Swartzentruber Amish, remain separate from more liberal districts, and when one of their number is hospitalized, they turn to each other for help. Neighbors give as they are able, the congregation chips in and holds fund-raisers, and the family makes small payments to the hospital and physician every month until the bill is paid off.

"Sometimes it takes years," says Dr. Elton Lehman, a Mount Eaton family physician who has a large Amish practice. He recalls a family who had a couple of premature babies when they lived in Michigan, and their bill at the children's hospital there was enormous. The family faithfully sent $25 a month to the hospital for many years until the bill was fully paid.

One Holmes County doctor says that his patients often make decisions on what level of care they will seek based on the anticipated cost and whether or not there's a reasonable hope for a good outcome.

"They don't do all the tests and procedures just for the sake of doing them," he says, noting that because they must pay their own hard-earned cash for their medical care, the Amish people are very cost-conscious consumers.

"The bottom line in all the plans," he says, "is that the Amish pay their bills. They take responsibility for their health care. What they don't do is stick healthcare providers with the bill."

They're extremely conscientious about paying their bills, agrees Rebecca Mutschelknause, the head of social services at Millersburg's Joel Pomerene Memorial Hospital, and that causes some difficulties occasionally.

"Our Amish patients will sometimes borrow money and pay interest on it in order to pay their doctor and hospital bills," she notes. "We try to tell them to make their payments directly to the hospital and doctors, because medical professionals don't charge interest."

The hospital social worker also agrees that her Amish clients are careful consumers, but she adds that they find themselves at the mercy of the healthcare system. While a very ill elderly person can choose to have his treatment limited or ended, where babies and children are concerned, the problem becomes a much more difficult matter of philosophy.

Explains Mutschelknause: "We as a society believe that all children need to come up perfect. When you're talking about the kind of care a two-pound 'preemie' needs, you're talking thousands of dollars a day for months."

Although finding a way to pay major medical bills is never easy, Mutschelknause and her colleagues at other area hospitals work with Amish patients and

their families to explore various options. The solution usually involves combining several different forms of community-based financial aid to help meet the expenses.

Purchasing commercial insurance may be taboo, and medical expenses are potentially very high, but Amish neighbors and families look after one another, and rely on divine mercy.

The philosophy is really very simple, according to one young woman: "We depend on God instead of money."

A Barn-Raising

An Amish barn-raising always draws a crowd — both workers and spectators. The photos on this page and the next three chronicle a barn-raising that took place at the Vernon Kline residence, west of Holmesville, in the spring of 1994.

A barn-raising is a community event for the Amish. Entire families pitch in to help — and to watch.

Page 102

Men and boys of all ages take part in the work. Sheer numbers help compensate for the lack of modern equipment.

Page 103

The bulk of the work is completed in one day. Below, you see how the Klines' new barn looked after the volunteers left.

CHURCH LEADERS CHOSEN BY LOTS

By Rhonda Rosner

No one asks for the positions of district preacher, deacon and bishop in the Amish church, and no one openly campaigns.

In fact, many times the "brothers" of the church are reluctant to be ordained, but because the church leaders are selected by "God's will," designated through "the casting of lots," they accept and commit themselves to their roles, an elderly New Order Amish bishop explains.

The eastern Holmes County man, who did not want to be identified, has served as bishop for a 30-family district for 17 years, and he was a preacher for many years before that. When new church leaders are needed, he says, each brother of the church who received at least three votes by church members must choose a hymnal from a line of them placed in front

of him. Each book is tied with a piece of string, which usually is unfastened by the bishop when the hymnal is selected by a nominee.

"A final decision has been made by God when a candidate selects the one book containing a piece of paper with the scripture from which this belief has been derived," the bishop says. The scripture is Acts 1:26. It says: "And they cast lots for them, and the lot fell on Matthias, and he was added to the eleven apostles."

Only preachers can be candidates for bishops. That selection is made in the same way — by casting lots.

Brothers of the Amish church realize that someday they may be called upon to be a minister. There is no monetary compensation for the church leaders. They maintain their every-day jobs, usually as farmers, carpenters or other craftsmen.

Preachers' duties are to lead the church and be in charge of weddings, funerals, communion and baptisms. There are two or three preachers in each Amish church district. Deacons are ordained as treasurers of the church.

Worship services are held every other Sunday. The bishop and preachers alternate giving the sermons. However, the bishop always leads the services.

The bishop bears more of the burden of responsibility than the other church members, and he has the final word when questions arise concerning the rules

of the church and the Amish way of life. His decisions, based on what the scripture says, are usually made after consultation with the members. Major decisions that could affect the Amish lifestyle are made only after serious debate among the bishops and ministers.

There is no special training required for ordination, but both preachers and bishops must devote a good deal of time to studying the Bible and memorizing scripture. Their chief responsibility, the Amish bishop says, is to be a good example.

Amish family and friends gather for the funeral of three of the children who were killed in the hit-run traffic accident.

Tragedy Accepted as God's Way

By Rhonda Rosner

In the wake of any tragedy, shock turns first to tears, then to strength as a community draws closer together to console itself in unified comfort.

But the Amish, in such circumstances, also rely on their faith.

The Amish believe that "God's hand" was involved in a recent accident that resulted in the death of five Amish children from three families.

Because "God could have protected the children, it must have been his will that it happened that way," said an elderly Old Order Amish bishop, who officiated at some of the funeral services.

The children, three of whom were from the same family, were walking home from a birthday party when they were struck and killed by a car that went out of control on Harrison Road, near Fredericksburg.

Another five youngsters were injured, three seriously, but they all recovered.

Although such a tragedy might seem insurmountable to some people, the Amish community continues to draw its strength from its faith, the bishop says.

"We've just got to turn it over to God. I'm in my 70s, and I know I don't know everything yet. It was a shock to everybody. It's one thing we can't realize until we're there."

The bishop, who has been a minister in his church for 38 years, says that most Amish in the area "don't bear a grudge" against the young man who drove the car.

"There's a prophet in the Bible that says our lives are hanging by a thread, and when the thread is cut, our lives are finished," the bishop says.

"It will take time to heal from this, but other people have hardships and deep sorrows, too," says Eli Miller, a neighbor of the three families.

"We're not angry at the man. We don't feel that way. We hope this will help him to maybe lead a better life later," Miller says. "It's sad to see families lose their children like that, but I guess it couldn't be helped. Our people feel that it was God's will — that God has his hand in there."

SHUNNING USED TO GUARD CULTURE

By Jeanine Kendle

A stirring incident that demonstrates the Old Order Amish society's desire to guard its customs was the celebrated "meidung," or shunning, case of 1947.

The incident resulted in a rare public trial that brought Amish life and religion to the scrutiny of the general public.

On March 24, 1947, an Amish farmer, Andrew J. Yoder, 32, filed a civil suit, in the Common Pleas Court of Wooster, against Old Order Amish Bishop John W. Helmuth; two preachers, John J. Nisley and Isaac I. Miller; and Deacon Emmanuel D. Wengerd.

Yoder sought $40,000 in damages and a court injunction against a boycott — a shunning — which he alleged had been organized against him throughout the Amish church.

One of Yoder's seven children had been afflicted

with polio at an early age in 1942, and it was necessary that she go to Wooster frequently for treatments. Because the rules of the church forbade Yoder to own and operate an automobile, the transportation problem of these weekly 30-mile roundtrips became formidable.

The Yoders thought they needed a car to provide their daughter the necessary treatments and a chance for normal existence. They withdrew from the Helmuth Amish congregation and became affiliated with a Conservative Amish group in the Bunker Hill district of Holmes County, which did not forbid the ownership of automobiles among its members.

The Yoders took this action in 1942. But the Old Order bishop, preachers and deacon would not tolerate the Yoders' withdrawal. Instead, they invoked Article 17 of the Dortrecht Confession of Faith — shunning — against Yoder in spite of the fact that he had not been expelled but had peacefully withdrawn from the church.

The meidung had been in effect for about five years in 1947. Yoder charged in his court suit that the purpose of the shunning or boycott was to compel him "to submit to church officials in the management of his trade, religious and business affairs, and it excluded him from all social and business relations with the members of said church by persuasion and intimidation."

His own brother, he said, had been requested to avoid him and to have no dealings with him, and his brother had been told that refusal to do so would place him under the ban and also make him an object of the boycott.

In addition, Yoder declared, the church authorities had approached his father to demand that he remove his son from the farm that he had been operating under lease from his father.

Yoder also listed other injurious instances of the application of the meidung.

At farm sales, old friends would speak, but then actually shun his company; at one funeral he had been forced to eat under an apple tree while the others dined in the house; at another, a farmer had requested that Yoder eat at a separate table in a corner of the room; at various threshings, he had been made to eat in the cellar.

Worst of all, he claimed, he had not been able to obtain help for his harvesting operations, and the men whom he did get to help were likewise banned from the church.

Yoder summed up the reasons for leaving the Old Order Amish church this way:

1. He had needed an automobile to afford transportation and to facilitate his farming operations.

2. He had needed transportation to Wooster, 15 miles distant, so that his daughter, crippled with

polio, might have treatments.

3. He had been opposed to the rule of his church, which prohibited male members from wearing rubber suspenders.

4. He had been against the boycott rule.

5. He had believed that he, too, had a natural and indefeasible right to worship God according to the dictates of his own conscience.

Yoder estimated that the damage to him, in injury of his own health and in isolation from society had amounted to some $40,000. He also asked that the defendants be immediately enjoined from continuing the boycott.

Yoder said he was forced to file the civil suit because he could find no other way out of the strict application of meidung, which had come to mean slow death for him in his rural setting. Many conferences had been held, previous to filing the suit, between him and Charles C. Jones, a former Wooster judge and Yoder's attorney, and Bishop Helmuth and other members of his district.

"We were trying to settle the matter in a peaceful way, as the Amish try to live, but the boycott, under church ruling, was 'for life' and everyone backed up the bishop," Jones said.

The conflict had reached a climax after Bishop Helmuth and Deacon Wengerd visited Yoder's father, Joseph.

What happened at that first meeting is not known. However, the two church officials returned two weeks later to see if the father had ousted his son from the farm. Yoder happened to be at his father's home on this occasion. Upon hearing how the bishop and deacon had tried to induce his father to drive him off the farm, Yoder became so angry that he grabbed the bishop by the beard and led him out of the door.

The first reply, carried in a local newspaper, to Yoder's court petition was from a spokesman for the Helmuth congregation. The reply called Yoder's accusations "one-sided and misrepresented." It asserted further that it had long been the practice of the church "to help get crippled children, as well as older people to the doctor or hospital by automobile or ambulance."

The reply denied that the boycott banned church members from exchanging work with the boycotted neighbor, and it added that Yoder's medical bills and other expenses could have been paid "had he remained faithful to the church."

Helmuth church officials would not, at first, file an official court answer; moreover, they refused to be represented by legal counsel. The reasons for this were that the very existence of the whole Old Order Amish church, not just of one individual Amish district, was at stake, they said, and the church had been

made the subject of an unwarranted attack.

The following letter appeared in the *Wooster Daily Record* of April 22, 1947:

"The Amish Church does not pretend to be a perfect church, as all of us make mistakes as well as everyone else. But as everyone knows, every church has rules and regulations which must be followed if we expect to keep up the rules of our forefathers as we believe should be done.

Our Christian forebears were drowned, hanged, burned alive and tortured in most brutal manners, but they did not hire lawyers to defend themselves. They stood for the truth, and the questions which they were asked they answered with the truth which they could do without the assistance of a lawyer. They depended upon the law and the rules that Christ gave them which reads: Matthew 10:17, "But beware of men; for they will deliver you up to the councils, and they will scourge you in their synagogue; 18, And ye shall be brought before governors and kings for my sake, for a testimony against them and the gentiles; 19, But when they deliver you up, take no thought what or how ye shall speak, for it shall be given you in that same you, what ye shall speak; 20, For it is not ye that speak, but the spirit of your Father which speaketh in you."

This we believe applies to any Christian people of today, the same as it did at that time when this law was given. We believe the honest kind of lawyers are perfectly right in their place and we can not do without them. But in a case like the Yoder case, where the lawyers are going to take over church matters, we have our Christian faith from our forefathers together with the laws of Christ. All we need to answer in this case is the truth — no matter what it leads up to — even imprisonment or fine.

Our forefathers came to America for freedom of religion — which we have had up to this time and with the Constitution of the United States, which now stands under law protecting freedom of religion, we shall be very thankful for, whenever our constitution to freedom of religion falls, our nation will also fall with it, according to the Bible."

However, the defendants subsequently indicated that they would file an answer to Yoder's charges, and they were given additional time by the court to prepare their reply.

At last, on May 3, 1947, Old Order church officials filed a reply — without representation by legal counsel. The defendants fully admitted putting Andrew J. Yoder under the ban, by citing Article 17 of the Confession of Dortrecht, and that thereby, he was shunned and boycotted by all faithful Amish.

They denied, however, some of the implications that Yoder had brought forth in his suit. The church leaders asserted that Yoder could not voluntarily leave the church without having the ban or boycott put on him.

On Nov. 5, 1947, the Common Pleas courtroom and galleries were filled to capacity; one sensed immediately that this was not an ordinary small-town trial.

The judge was Walter J. Mougey, of Alsatian Mennonite descent. The 12 jurors, nine men and three women, were all from outside of Wooster. The bishop, preachers and deacon did not have legal counsel. To the last, it was doubted whether they would appear in court at all. No notes, no papers, no documents marked them as participants.

The Amish leaders passed among themselves a worn, coverless Bible and a diminutive pocket edition of the Dortrecht Confession of Faith. They were not familiar with court procedure, and the judge reminded them frequently of their privilege to ask questions of Yoder's witnesses.

Among the 12 witnesses were: Yoder's wife; Sarah Mellot; Yoder's aged father, Joseph; and his elder brother, Dan. Frequent flashes of photographers' bulbs made the defendants cringe and hide their faces.

The attorneys pointed out that this suit was not an action against any church, but it so happened that all the defendants were members of the Old Order Amish faith.

Bishop Helmuth's rebuttal address to the jury was brief: "I am sorry that this occasion is on hand. We feel that we will stand on Articles 16 (excommunication from the church) and 17 (shunning) of the Confession of Faith, written in Dortrecht, Holland, in 1632."

The four defendants were the first to take the witness chair. The questioning revolved around mainly establishing an affirmative answer on two points:

- Did the defendants put the ban on Andy Yoder and on others who would not boycott Yoder?
- Did the four defendants know at the time of placing the ban on the plaintiff that he had an invalid daughter whose plight necessitated his buying a car and having to withdraw from his original congregation?

The testimony of defendants and other witnesses to these questions seemed incontrovertible and corroborated the original charge.

The defendants were reluctant to answer. Their most common remarks were: "We have nothing to say," or, "The Confession of Faith," or, "The Bible."

They had to admit, however, that they had put the ban on Andy Yoder. They displayed an unshakable belief in the "Christian-ness" and righteousness of the meidung practice of their church.

They tried to justify their actions by the fact that it was done for the good of Yoder's soul.

When Yoder's attorney asked, "What if Andy's soul had gone in this state to its maker?", the audience was amused, but Bishop Helmuth refused to

answer. Later, however, the bishop interrupted with the remark: "We ought to obey God more than man."

It was clearly established that Yoder's sin was his departure from the Old Order Amish group. Only repentance and a return to the habits and customs of the original flock could atone for this, the church leaders said. Amish friends of Yoder who had refused to shun him and had, therefore, been excommunicated had been reinstated to full membership upon repentance and confession of their wrongdoings.

Final arguments were offered on the afternoon of the second day. All four defendants took advantage of the privilege to address the jury in their own behalf. They expressed their regret that this case had come to court; all four of them were close to tears as they quoted the "Law of God" in support of shunning and excommunication as prescribed in the Confession of Faith.

"We are God-fearing men," preacher Nicely said, "and what I believe, I can't change. If Andy Yoder's defiance of the church laws in the use of an automobile to carry an invalid daughter to a doctor had been a brother sin between Andy and me, we might have made it up. But when Andy went down on his knees and confessed in baptism all this (the Confession of Faith) to be right, we had nothing else to do with it. The matter is between Andy and God; I am praying to God that the church and the jury do right. I am grateful that we have an order like this court. We also must have that kind of order in the church."

The next day the judge gave the jury its instructions, and it went into deliberations. Within an hour and 25 minutes the jury returned a unanimous verdict for Yoder, awarding him $5,000 damages.

In connection with the verdict, the judge ordered the four church men to abandon their boycott against Andy Yoder and granted the injunction restraining them from imposing any boycott against Andy Yoder that would deny him the right to religious liberty or deprive him of any business or social relations with his fellow church members. The judge also ordered church officials to withdraw any order instructing their congregation to boycott Yoder for alleged violation of church rules.

Yoder's comment when interviewed after the conclusion of his suit was: "I am satisfied. I believe the injunction will do more good than the damages. I think they (the church men) will think some time before they put on any more bans."

But the case was not actually settled in court. Its true conclusion came months later. Yoder had won a verdict from the Amish leaders awarding him $5,000 in damages, but these leaders always had contended that the affair was God's doing, and since the worldly powers had interfered and decided the matter, they, themselves, would do nothing further about it. The

verdict was not appealed, but neither were steps taken to comply with the court order.

Toward the end of December 1947, Sheriff Wayne Warner of Holmes County was ordered to execute a sale of the chattel property of Bishop John Helmuth. The farm and land on which Helmuth lived were not included in the court action because the land was under mortgage.

After appraisals . . . a great crowd of people, buyers, curious spectators and newspapermen alike gathered on the premises of the Helmuth farm, located just south of Mount Eaton in Holmes County. The bishop had left the scene early in the morning, but his wife and daughter had remained to witness the sale, which impoverished them.

The sheriff's report of the sale showed the exact items sold, including 226 items with 31 sums of money received. The larger amounts showed that eight hogs brought $550; 130 shocks of corn, $91; the bishop's surrey brought $36, after spirited bidding by two graybeards, one of whom was related to the bishop; another buggy sold for $41; two Holstein cows, $150; one Jersey cow, $85; three horses, $100; a mower for $35.

The total amount raised was $2,359.61, which after the deduction of costs left a total of $2,276.51 to be credited to the $5,000 judgment.

A month later, the sheriff's department started listing the chattel property of preacher John Nisley.

But suddenly there came a surprising, dramatic action. On Jan. 29, 1948, Nisley appeared in the sheriff's office with $2,939.04 in cash — the exact amount needed to complete the claim. He made no comment on how he secured the money or why he had taken steps to comply with the judgment, but his actions came a week after four Amish church officials from Lancaster County, Pa., had visited Wooster to examine court records and hold conferences with various Amish leaders, Bishop Helmuth and Andy Yoder.

To the amusement of a few observers, these men from Pennsylvania, had twice come in a rented motor vehicle — although possession of an automobile was as sinful for them as it was for the Ohio Amish.

The small girl whose illness precipitated the quarrel among church members died at the home of her parents, after a brief illness, on April 4, 1949. She was 7.

Editor's note: Information for this article was taken from the book "Our Amish Neighbors," published in 1962 and written by William I. Schreiber, a long-time German professor at The College of Wooster.

Section IV
Growing Up

Separate Schools Serve Amish Youth

By Rhonda Rosner

The first bell peals out its warning that school is about to start, and groups of Holmes County Amish children hasten their steps toward the one-room parochial schoolhouse nearest their homes.

The children appear to be in a collectively cheerful mood, laughing and talking among themselves, swinging their lunch buckets and occasionally waving to a passer-by. In fall or spring, if the weather is warm, they may be barefoot, and the boys will be wearing broad-rimmed straw hats. For early arrivals, a quick game of softball might fill the time before school is called to session.

In winter, the children, cheeks reddened by the brisk, cold air, will be bundled in heavy, dark clothing, including scarves, bonnets and stocking caps. If there is snow, sleds are dragged along to school in

anticipation of some fun at recess.

Cloaks, coats and hats are hung on hooks, and the youngsters, ranging from first- to eighth-graders, seated at their desks, respond "good morning" to roll call, then in unison bow their heads to pray "The Lord's Prayer."

A similar scene is repeated daily, August to April, by the 1,735 Amish students who attend the 56 Amish parochial schools in Holmes County — mostly in the eastern portion of the county.

The Amish community supports these private schools in the belief that a parochial education that focuses on a basic curriculum "fits in better to our way of living," according to Emanuel Erb, one of a three-member advisory committee for his Amish school district.

An eighth-grade education — or attendance until the 14th birthday, whichever comes first — is considered "adequate" and usually marks the end of an Amish student's educational career, according to Erb, who has four children in the parochial system.

"We think it's important to stick to the basics — reading, comprehension, writing skills, arithmetic, English and we have our own German classes. Religious training from the teacher is just to be a good example. Otherwise, we leave that to home and church," Erb says.

The Amish school advisory committee is composed of a representative from each of three area districts: North, covering Wayne and Stark counties; Middle, for Holmes and surrounding counties north of Ohio 39; and South, Holmes and surrounding counties south of Ohio 39. Members are elected to six-year terms.

One of the duties of the committee, Erb says, is to spend five days each year visiting the different schools. Each year, about 40 of the 100 buildings in the three-district area are inspected.

"We look to see what the teachers are doing, what the curriculum is and if there are any questions," Erb says.

The advisory committee meets annually with committees from the individual schools to discuss problems or special issues.

Buildings, which are the property of the church and its respective school district, are heated by wood, coal or natural gas, and each building is maintained by its own five- or three-member school board. Board members are elected by the persons in the individual school districts. A clerk maintains all records. The board is also responsible for hiring the teacher. Most of the teachers are members of the Amish community.

"Ninety-five percent are among our own people. We ask that they be members in good standing with the church and have the ability to get along with chil-

dren," Erb says.

Training sessions for new teachers are held during the summer at the schools. The are led by experienced teachers. Erb, who served as a parochial teacher at one time, says the majority of the teachers are young Amish women.

The number of teachers varies with the enrollment, which averages between 20 and 50 students, he says. Schools with 35 or more students generally have two teachers, and in some schools, the teacher has an assistant, usually a 15- or 16-year-old girl.

The teachers play a major part in planning the curriculum, according to Erb. Texts and workbooks are obtained through the Pathway Co., a book supplier in Ontario, Canada, and the Gordonville Print Shop in Pennsylvania. Sometimes the teachers supply some of their own books. All school materials and books are subject to the advisory committee's approval.

Although a few of the buildings have two rooms, most have only one, which is sometimes divided in half by a curtain. The buildings are constructed of wood, bricks or blocks, and although some have been built to serve the Amish community, others were once one-room public schools.

Students who come from as far as five miles away travel by bicycle or buggy, but most are within walking distance of the schools.

A bell, secured in the tower of each school building, rings first at 8 a.m. and students begin to arrive. A typical five-hour school day is in session by 8:30, with singing and devotions among the first orders of business.

Erb recalls that in his classroom, reading and arithmetic were the first lessons conducted. Reading lessons for the lower grades followed recess, then math and reading for the upper classes until lunchtime, which is usually at 11:30 a.m.

"Everybody brings their own," Erb says. "After lunch, our goal usually was to play a game where everyone could be involved, like running games or softball. Sometimes there are two diamonds — one is for the younger ones. Whenever the weather permits, we're outside. We think fresh air and exercise are what the children need."

Next, the students are treated to a story — an interesting one with a good moral lesson, Erb says. Storytime gives the students a chance to relax for 10 to 15 minutes before geography or history lessons begin.

Because students come up in groups to a table at the front, it's sometimes difficult to concentrate when other classes are reciting, but the other students soon learn to adjust, Erb says. Except during German lessons, English is spoken at school.

"When you're teaching eight grades, there's not much time. You have to keep things running," the

former instructor says.

Maintaining discipline is important in the schools, and "as a rule, there are no problems with parents supporting the teacher," Erb says.

School, usually conducted five days a week, begins about the last week in August and ends in mid or late April, interrupted only by Thanksgiving, Christmas, Old Christmas (Jan. 6) and sometimes New Year's Day. Good Friday is also a vacation day if it falls during the school year.

Amish Teacher Describes School

By John Roepke

The Amish system of educating their children is not that different from the English system, despite what people may think, one former parochial teacher says.

Dennis Kline, 37, an Amishman who recently retired after 16 years of teaching, says that Amish children receive a quality education, one that is comparable to that of a child who is not Amish.

"Through eighth grade, I think it's comparable. As far as teaching the basics, I don't think there's a big difference."

Kline doesn't feel the Amish school system should be reformed because it works well the way it is.

"We generally feel that a higher education is not going to do us a lot of good. Although I feel it's important to get a basic education, and if someone

wants to pursue a certain field, they're able . . . to do it. We like to say that we're equipping them to study if they want to take a specialized study of something."

There is no standard board of education for Amish schools, as is customary in the public-education system, Kline says. Each schoolhouse has a three-member board that supervises and runs it independently. Still, the curriculum and what the children are taught doesn't vary that much.

One reason is most teachers use the same textbooks. This makes the curriculum more uniform. Still, it ultimately is up to the teacher to decide what he or she will teach, Kline says.

And unlike public school systems, there is no certification process required to become a teacher in an Amish school. But, Kline says, the boards try to get teachers they feel will do a good job.

The Amish have their own school system so they can teach their children in ways that reflect their beliefs, he says.

"We feel we should have control over our children. Keep them it an environment with a Christian influence.

"Also, there are things like evolution. We teach creation. We believe that because the Bible says it. We don't use the Bible as a textbook, but we try to teach biblical principles in school."

The influence of religion is probably the biggest difference between the Amish parochial schools and the public schools, he says.

"We have morning devotions. We read out of the Bible and pray. We feel the church needs to be involved in a school because we want to train and teach our children in the right way."

If there is a weak point to the Amish educational system, Kline says, it's that the parents don't get more involved in school.

"I wish we could get parents more involved in the school and see the importance of education more than they do."

School for Amish children starts at 8:30 a.m. and ends at 3 p.m. There are four class periods, each 75 minutes long. The students have an hour for lunch and two 15-minute recess periods.

School starts at the end of August and goes to the end of April, Kline says. Depending on how many snow days there are, the children will attend school for 160 days each year.

"Although, it has to be a pretty bad snowstorm before we'll have a snow day," he says. "If it's 20-below zero, we probably won't have school."

Most Amish children start school when they are 6 years old and graduate when they are 14, says Kline, who started teaching when he was 20. The highest grade in an Amish school is the eighth.

Most of the schools have all eight grades in one classroom, which works out well unless one class is a particularly large one, he says. The average size of a school is about 25 children.

There are probably 50 Amish parochial schools in Holmes County, he estimates, and there are approximately 10 male teachers in the county.

"I wouldn't say it's rare. But I suppose men are outnumbered 10 to one."

Kline says there isn't much difference between male and female teachers in his eyes, and he doesn't feel he gets treated any differently because he's a man.

"I know people get the idea that a male teacher is better," he says. "But for myself, I don't think there's a great deal of difference."

A typical course load in Kline's last school, located near Holmesville, included: arithmetic, English, German, reading, spelling, geography, vocabulary and composition.

Not every class is taught each day, he says. Some, like geography and composition, are taught on a less frequent basis than English and arithmetic, which are taught daily.

German is taught so the children don't forget their heritage and so they can read and understand it. But other courses are taught in English, he says, and students have to speak English when they're in school.

"They need the English to get along in today's world. If you're not fluent in English, you're going to suffer. All the newspapers and books, everything, is in English. You talk with English people, and so we consider it important to be fluent in English.

"In fact, we have the pupils speak English at all times, so they learn to speak it properly. If we don't enforce that, they'll speak German and they'll never master English."

School is probably the only place the children will speak English while they are young, he says, but after a while it becomes automatic to them.

Kline considers reading the most important subject for the students, especially the ones in the lower grades.

"If they master reading, there are very few other subjects that are not connected to that. A good reader has a good start."

Kline compares learning how to read and write to an apprentice carpenter. If the teacher just shows the apprentice what to do but doesn't let him actually do any work, when the time comes for the apprentice to build something, he won't know how to apply what he's been taught, he says.

During math class, the Amish schools stick with the basics. They don't teach the more complex courses like trigonometry and calculus.

"We get into algebra. We scratch the surface in

eighth grade. That's about as far as we go."

Amish students learn both United States and world geography, and as much local geography as possible. The children also are taught U. S. history, even though Kline says it isn't "the same hero-worshipping style" the English children learn.

"We touch it so they at least know our country's basic heritage. We don't try to make heroes out of the early pioneers, but teach them who did what."

Surprisingly, the Amish schools don't teach a lot of Amish church history, though Kline says he would like to see some taught.

"Actually, I think it would be a fairly good idea if we taught them some church history."

The curriculum focuses on what the students will need to use most in their lives, Kline says.

"Especially when we get into eighth grade, there are some sections that we dwell much longer on, but they're going to use them more."

One of the biggest problems is teacher turnover, Kline says. Students rarely have the same teacher for their entire school career.

"A lot of times we have teachers, maybe young girls in their late teens and early 20s, and a lot of them get married and quit teaching," he says. "That's one reason. It seems like most of the time (the students) won't have the same teacher."

His students will have a new teacher next semester.

He has retired from teaching at Shady Grove School after spending five years there.

"I needed a break. There are some reasons — mainly I just got tired of the stress of it. Also the financial part of it. It's hard to raise a family on a teacher's wages."

Kline is married and has four children, ranging in age from 8 months to 7 years. The family lives near

The end of another school day seems to bring joy to all kids.

Holmesville.

Kline taught at his first school for eight years. He quit that job because he got married and moved farther away from the school.

"It just wasn't practical" to teach at the school, he says.

He then went to another school about three miles from his home, and stayed there for three years. When the job opened at Shady Grove, which is about a mile up the road from his home, he took it.

"I always thought I'd kind of like to teach. I enjoyed school when I went to school. I enjoy bookwork and I like children. It's kind of natural for me."

'CITY' TEACHERS LIKE THE AREA, TOO

By Kevin Lynch

Relocating to Holmes County from the Cleveland area is a major change not only in scenery — trading skyscrapers for barns — but in the culture as well.

For Cathie Lynch and Julie Purdy, elementary art teachers in the East Holmes School District, teaching in rural communities is a far cry from the city districts where they received their training.

"In a way, it was like coming home for me," Purdy says. She received her training and did her student teaching in Akron, but she spent her first few years of school in Uniontown-Hartville, an Amish community in Stark County.

"I found it really neat that I went to school with Amish, and then here I am teaching them," Purdy said.

Both teachers agree that teaching Amish children

has been much more enjoyable than their experience in the big city.

"I still remember when I came down for my job interview at the central office," Lynch recalls. "When I got out of the car and heard the cows mooing, I couldn't believe it."

Lynch says just getting to work is more enjoyable

This one-room Amish school is near New Bedford.

because of the lovely countryside.

"The beautiful scenery here is a lot better than the ride I had to work in Cleveland. It wasn't much fun sitting in rush-hour traffic for more than an hour sometimes.

"And although the schedule is a little harder than what I had in Cleveland, it is easier to get the job

done because there are fewer discipline problems," Lynch says.

Purdy reports few discipline problems as well. She credits the strong family unit in the district for the well-behaved children.

"Family is very important. The family and community are very supportive of education, making our jobs so much more pleasant," she says.

The fact that Amish kindergarten students come to school speaking only German causes problems at first, but eventually the teachers are able to work their way past the language barrier.

"I've never really had a problem," Purdy says. "I was taking a sign language course when I started teaching here, and I was able to use those visualization skills to reach the students. Fortunately, art is a visualization subject."

BOYS BECOME MEN AT AGE 14

By Kevin Lynch

For most 14-year-old boys, life is hard enough when you consider the physical and emotional changes that take place as boys become young men.

But for the Amish, 14 is the age when most boys finish their schooling and enter the working world.

It is a time of great change, but for most of these young men, it is a welcome time in their lives.

"I'm just glad it's my eighth year," says Leroy Yoder, an eighth-grade student at Mount Hope Elementary School. "I'm glad to be out of here."

Leroy says he will help his father on the family's small dairy farm when he is through with school. He has been preparing for this by helping out on the farm.

"It's my job to feed the calves," Leroy says. "When I go home from school, I usually read a little and do

Amish boys learn how to take care of horses at an early age.

my homework. Then, I'll help my dad, eat and then go to bed."

He says he doesn't expect his life will change too much once he's out of school.

Marty Raber, also 14, is a classmate of Leroy's. He says his average day is a lot like Leroy's.

"I go home do the chores, help dad, eat supper and then do my homework," Marty says. "And I like to play sports. I like basketball. And I also play a little pitch and catch. I also like to read."

Marty plans to go to work in his father's furniture business when he is through with school.

Leroy says he likes to hunt, especially for deer, squirrel and rabbits when he's not working.

Merlin Miller, another classmate, says he'll probably go to work for his father in the family's home-improvement business.

Sledding seems to have universal appeal.

"I've been going along with my dad in the summers to help out, and that's probably what I'm going to do when I'm through with school," Merlin says.

He likes to play basketball and softball when he gets the chance, he says.

Vernon Raber, also 14, is another classmate who is looking forward to the end of the school year so he can go to work on the family farm.

When he's not working, Vernon likes any kind of sports. "I especially like to hunt and fish," he says.

The boys all agree that girls are not yet part of the picture.

"Girls are definitely out of the question," Vernon says. At least for the time being.

Girls Like to Have Fun, Too

By Rhonda Rosner

Girls will be girls.

Amish girls, just like their "English" counterparts, enjoy getting together with their friends, playing games and sometimes doing things that are just a little outrageous.

Anita Miller, 13, the daughter of Dan and Betty Miller of Millersburg, recently finished her formal, full-time education when she went through eighth-grade graduation at Chestnut Ridge School.

Anita, who will work this summer baby-sitting and cleaning houses, is considering taking a business course this fall. The course, offered in the East Holmes School District, is geared toward preparing Amish teenagers for jobs following completion of the eighth grade. She isn't interested in a secretarial job, but would like to be a store clerk, she says.

Anita, who considers herself an average student, says she enjoyed school, but she is looking forward to going on to other things. Her favorite class was history, and her most difficult were math and English.

However, the Chestnut Ridge graduate says she will miss the routine of school and seeing her classmates every day, especially close friends like Marilyn Garber, who lives in Walnut Creek.

A typical day for Anita begins about 6:30 a.m. Her first job is to prepare breakfast for her family while her 12-year-old brother, Tim, feeds the heifers and horses. Evening milking begins soon after school. Anita assists her father with this two-hour chore, while her mother prepares supper.

After the meal, there is time for other interests. Anita, who makes her own dresses, enjoys sewing and reading.

Because she is a "morning person," Anita also rises early on Saturdays and helps with the housecleaning until lunch time. She fills her free time with sewing and cross-stitching. On Sundays, she attends church with her family and spends the afternoon visiting.

Anita says she has never thought of her life as "inconvenient" even without modern luxuries. Her home is powered by a generator, has gas lights and an indoor bathroom.

Teenage Amish girls enjoy getting together to giggle, gossip and eat a lot of things that can cause tooth decay at sleep-overs — very much like the traditional slumber parties of their "English" counterparts.

Amish girls don't watch TV or movies, but most other slumber-party traditions are observed. Anita says that she and her friends fix their hair, eat candy and chips, and play games such as table tennis during sleep-overs.

The girls like to dare each other to do amusing, but not too harmful stunts, such as painting their fingernails pink, acting like a "drunk rooster," standing on their heads or saying "Yeah, right" to a teacher the next day in class. A party-goer who falls asleep may awaken with a shoe on her face.

During one of their parties, the girls had enough energy left at 2 a.m. to go outside and jump on the trampoline.

Anita enjoys basketball and softball, and pitch-and-catch with her brother, who is good company "if he's in a good mood," she says. Her other interests include horseback riding, shopping and taking walks and buggy rides with her friends.

Like most other teenagers, Anita and her friends love to ride the rollercoasters at Cedar Point. The Wildcat is her personal favorite. The highlight of her final schoolyear was a field trip to the amusement park, which she also has visited with her family.

Anita will be allowed to date when she turns 18. She says there is "someone" she likes now, but she's

not divulging any secrets. Someday, she says she would like to get married and have a family, perhaps with three children.

If she were to travel in the future, Anita says she would like to go to Switzerland to see the mountains or to Australia, which she says "seems like it is in the middle of nowhere and not really connected to any other country."

Inspired by a visit to an aunt at Virginia Beach, Va., Anita also says she would like to go to Florida, to the beach. Her goal is to work in voluntary service, following in the footsteps of her sister, Rosie, who works at the Faith Mission Home in Virginia.

If she could have the world her way, Anita Miller says she would free it of crime and "give a home to the poor and food to the hungry."

Marilyn Garber, left, and Anita Miller

THERE'S TIME FOR GAMES

By Kevin Lynch

Venturing through the back roads of Holmes County, it is not uncommon to see a group of Amish children playing a game out in the yard. The games they play are not much different than the yard games the "English" play.

On most summer days, the schoolyards are filled with softball players and the parking lots are filled with buggies. Softball is one of the most popular games played, but most yards aren't big enough for fielding a game, so schoolyards or parks are often the field of dreams for Amish baseball players.

A group of Amish boys recently took time between innings of a softball game at Wise School in Holmes County to talk about their favorite games.

"Softball is my favorite game," said James, a 14-year-old. "I'm pretty good, too. But I like to play

other games, too."

He said he also likes to play volleyball and soccer.

"I like to play softball and volleyball," said Jonas, also 14. "I don't have much time to play, so I have to enjoy it while I can."

The boys said their work regimen at home doesn't allow for much fun time.

"I like to play catch with my brother when I can't play a game," James added. "We make our own games while playing catch."

The Amish boys aren't the only ones who get to

Boys and girls both participate in a schoolyard softball game.

participate in games.

Ann, a 14-year-old Amish girl, said girls like to play games, too.

"We like to play kick ball and soccer. I'm not very good at softball, but we'll play catch sometimes."

One of the most popular yard games is volleyball.

"The kids love to play volleyball because it is such a fast game," said one Amish woman in attendance at the softball game. "When I was a kid, we used to play croquet. That used to be the more popular game. But it is not fast enough for the kids."

Croquet is still popular among the Amish, but it is played more by the adults than their children.

Despite differences, one thing that bridges many cultures is athletics, and that is evident by the fact that Amish children enjoy playing the same games as their English counterparts.

Section V
Making A Living

Rising Land Prices Bring Changes

By Amelia T. Reiheld

Until just a generation ago, almost any young Amish man could count on spending his life farming. It kept him close to home and community, close to the earth and a quiet and stable life, and close to his God.

Farming came naturally to the Amish. Their Swiss-German ancestors worked the soil, as did those who migrated to America's heartland. Their large families and close-knit church communities made it possible to farm in the old ways, with horse-drawn plows and without much hired help. Maintaining farms in keeping with tradition made it easier to live and raise families in the old ways, thus avoiding a cultural drift toward modern habits and a worldly lifestyle.

Although they still live in traditional Amish households, more and more of the community's young

people are looking away from the farm for their livelihood — not so much as a choice, but as a matter of necessity. It's almost impossible, agree several Mount Hope residents, for a young person to set up farming, unless he inherits the family farm.

Paul Yoder, the manager of Lehman's Hardware in Mount Hope, explains that agricultural equipment, even that of the horse-drawn variety, is very expensive. The cost of Holmes County farmland is almost prohibitive — from $3,000 to $6,000 an acre or more, according to Yoder. Industry, tourism and expanding suburbia all serve to drive up the price of what was once agricultural land.

When a farm comes on the market, it is often carved up into smaller plots, which can be sold far more profitably for commercial or residential development.

While Amish farmers rarely are willing to sell their farms for development, still, within a large Amish family, there may be half a dozen boys who are potential farmers. Who gets the farm?

It varies. Not every child wants to farm, of course. The older boys are ready to earn a living long before their parents are ready to retire. With them, the choice, as Yoder points out, is to "get a day job or move outside the community," to a locale where land prices are lower.

Often, it's the youngest son who inherits the family

farm. He grows up helping out with the chores, and by the time he's old enough to think about wanting a farm of his own, his parents are beginning to want to slow down.

Farming is a tough way to make a living. Yoder puts it succinctly: "The price of milk has dropped, but the price of groceries never falls."

Older children of Amish families, then, must earn a living away from the family farm. Many boys work as hired hands on a neighbor's farm for a few years after they leave school at age 13 or 14. By age 16 or 17, they often also have developed usable skills as carpenters, woodworkers or shopkeepers. By then, they're old enough to find a job operating heavy factory equipment. The girls often help out at home with younger children or work for family friends and neighbors. When they're a little older, they'll clean houses or work in nearby shops, restaurants, factories and nursing homes.

Finding work is seldom a problem for the Amish, even with their limited formal education.

"There are not enough good people to go around. Anyone who's willing to work can find work," says Yoder, noting that the local grapevine is the most effective way of matching workers to jobs. "They tell me that this county has the lowest unemployment and the lowest average wage of any in Ohio. We're a self-supporting community. If you can't find it in

Holmes County, you just can't find it."

While most non-farming Amish folk are employed in area industries or small companies, many are establishing their own businesses and cottage industries. Some cater to needs within the community, such as harness-making, buggy repair and bulk foods. Furniture-making has become a major source of jobs in the area, as woodworking shops produce chairs, cabinetry and garden furniture for sale by much larger companies. Others are little home-based businesses that have sprung up to attract the attention of a growing number of "English" passers-by. Small signs by the roadside offer baked goods, farm produce and hand-crafted gifts to tourists.

Many of the women enjoy gathering for quilting bees to produce traditional hand-crafted wallhangings and bedspreads. Long a Holmes County specialty, this beautiful needlework recently has found its way to a larger market. Sarah Yoder, of the Lone Star Quilt Shop in Mount Hope, coordinates the sale of handmade Amish quilts through an internationally known catalog store.

There's a secret to starting up a small business and making it prosper, says Ervin Yoder, whose harness-repair shop also sells shoes and sundry dry goods. In addition to Sarah's large quilt shop in the back of the store, the family operates a furniture store as well. "The secret is to start slow, with a small shop, and

then work into it. It takes sometimes two or three years before you can afford to go full-time."

His advice to would-be entrepreneurs? Don't quit your day job — at least not right away.

Although Old Order church members don't have telephones or electric appliances in their houses, nor do they own automobiles, there's no prohibition against using power tools when they're working for other people, and many jobs require it.

While Ervin Yoder says the church sets no specific guidelines for what jobs are appropriate and which aren't, "we don't recommend working at a place with a lot of foul language or drinking, or where it's a bad influence."

Working "outside" has forced the Amish to come to terms with cultural institutions that run counter to their inclinations. The biblical instruction to keep themselves separate from the rest of the world becomes ever more difficult for Amish families. The scarcity of farmland and the necessity for working outside the Amish community inevitably brings with it an exposure to outside pressures and temptations, and an emphasis on making money that wasn't part of the old way.

The influx of tourists to the area not only has brought further economic pressure to develop farmland into shopping areas and tourist attractions, but has turned the Amish themselves into objects of pub-

lic curiosity.

"What's happening here is the same thing that's happened in Pennsylvania," Ervin Yoder says.

As Holmes County land prices continue to rise, those who move away from the area to continue farming, find themselves cut off from the close-knit family and community support of their childhood. These dilemmas worry many of the older Amish folk, who remember a very different world only a couple of decades earlier. They can't help but wonder what will become of their children — and their children's children.

Although times may be difficult for those whose plain way of life depends to a large degree upon isolation from a hectic world, the way is clear to Ervin Yoder: "We'll just keep trying to follow the example that Jesus left."

Selling Land Hurts the Amish

By Rhonda Rosner

It's almost like losing a member of the family.

That's the analogy an Amish farmer uses to describe the recent sale of 47 acres of his 138.5-acre farm.

"I kind of struggled with this. If you're a true-blooded farmer, the farm becomes a part of you. The farmer is not a speculator. Therefore, selling land or part of a farm is like going through a divorce or a death in the family," he says.

The property was subdivided into five- to 11-acre "mini farms," according to the Amishman, who preferred that his name not be used. The market value was greater if the land was offered in larger parcels because it left more potential for the buyers, he says.

The dairy farmer says he became concerned about housing developments encroaching on his property

when his cousin moved his family to Ashtabula County and put 15 acres up for sale. That acreage bordered the farmer's shop, barn and house.

"I already knew someone was interested in buying it and splitting it up in lots. Would you want that? So I bought it. It belonged to my grandfather originally, and I didn't want to see it split up. I moved my shop here."

The Amishman supplements his farm income with a wood-working and furniture shop.

"I really didn't want to see it (the 47-acre tract) become a development. The bottom line is, I'm a farmer. I have two sons on the farm. We pride ourselves on our property, and we'd like to pass it on to the next generation and hope it provides a living for them."

The third generation to live on and farm the property, the Amishman still has not sold "one inch of the original family farm," he says. The tract he sold was additional acreage that was purchased in 1981 and 1988.

"This is taking place nationally due to the farm economy," the Amishman says. "My first preference was to expand the farm so that a son or daughter could make a living from it, but farm prices (for commodities) have been depreciating every year. Milk prices are essentially what they were 15 years ago and still declining."

Unfortunately, farming is unique because rising (land) prices are not reflected in farmers' incomes, he says.

"Did your last pair of shoes cost more or less? See what we're facing? Farm equipment costs a good bit more than it did 10 years ago."

The farmer, a member of the Beachy Order of Amish, says several neighbors who had milking herds five years ago now are out of the business.

That trend is a harbinger of the demise of the American family farm, he predicts bleakly.

"I say, regretfully, that in the future we'll see more of this. I don't like to see it. Farmland is being used up to an extent we never even realized. The way the farm economy is now, we have to increase units of production to stay in business. It's endless.

"We, as a family, decided we didn't want more cows. Where would it end? We decided we had some land that had real market potential. We could offer it for auction and see what happens."

The seven parcels of land were sold at auction in 1994 to young couples, including a niece and her husband. The new owners, both Amish and non-Amish, currently are building houses or are in the process of moving into their newly constructed homes.

The Amishman says he has managed to maintain the same number of cows (60) on the reduced acreage. He has no plans for "major changes" on the

rest of the farm, except, perhaps, to build a retirement home for his own use.

The furniture shop is a family project, he says. "I like to be family-oriented."

Many young Amish would prefer to farm, but instead, are turning to trades and skilled crafts such as carpentry, he says.

"What's happening is affecting the Amish people. With a job, about all the investment needed is a lunch bucket. The wages that can be earned are beyond what agriculture can offer. The agricultural community cannot compete with a salary, and that is one influence that is drawing the younger generation from farming."

The changing farm economy is having a negative effect on the Amish culture, the Amishman says.

"We, as rural people, are victims of circumstances beyond our control."

Families Join to Grow Produce

By Rhonda Rosner

Thirty acres in eastern Holmes County — tilled, planted and harvested by 15 Amish families — produce enough vegetables to provide 45 Ohio supermarkets and wholesalers with locally grown produce.

Green bell peppers is the specialty crop of this group of Holmes County Amish farmers, who have developed a strong commercial market for their pickles, cucumbers, yellow zucchini, eggplants, tomatoes, butternut and acorn squash, green beans and some hot peppers.

According to one of the farmers, when the idea originated, only three families were involved. The goal of the project was to provide profitable work at home for family members and educate the children in a valuable trade.

The first step toward sowing that first seed was to

obtain information and growing tips from the Holmes County Extension Service office, after which, the farmers established a cooperative marketing group.

During the next few years, other Amish families in the area expressed an interest in marketing produce, and the business expanded to the present 15 growers, who supply the hand labor necessary for the planting, weeding and harvesting.

"We felt (if the business expanded) we could give more people a chance to get started growing produce," says the farmer, who was one of the founders

An Amishman sells some produce while relaxing under a shade tree.

of the business. "And if we could pool together, we could haul bigger loads, greater distances.

"By increasing the number of growers, of course, we needed additional markets, which is seemingly no problem for a high-quality, home-grown product. Supermarkets seem very willing to buy local Holmes County products."

An increase in volume during the last several years created a need for a centralized packing plant, which is located north of Berlin, off County Road 207. There, eight employees grade, pack and cool the produce before shipping.

The group employs only one truck to deliver the produce to the stores and warehouses. Some wholesalers pick up the produce at the packing house.

A committee is in charge of quality control and getting the bedding plants.

"We're careful to choose greenhouses that are clean and disease-free," the farmer says. "We try to advise and educate new growers and help them get started."

Insects are controlled through an integrated pest-management program, he says. A scout inspects the fields once a week, keeping a close eye on the plants for disease and insects. Based on week-to-week records, the farmers determine the amount of chemical spray necessary to protect the crop.

"It's impossible not to use any chemicals at all," the farmer says, but the pest management program helps reduce their use.

"We work closely with the county Extension office on the spraying," he says, "carefully following the directions on any product we use."

Although a waterwheel transplanter is used, each plant has to be set in the soil by hand, the Amish farmer explains. The transplanter punches holes in plastic sheets, placed in rows over the crops to inhibit weeds and maintain moisture and heat in the soil.

A trickle irrigation system keeps the plants fertilized and watered by using thin, punctured plastic tubes run under the plastic sheets. The water, filtered first, comes from nearby ponds or creeks.

During peak weeks each year, the growers produce approximately 1,100 bushels of bell peppers, the farmer says.

CATERING HELPS FAMILY SURVIVE

By A. Nicole Springfield

A Baltic area Amish family that opened its dining room to a group of out-of-town employees working in the area has ended up serving busloads of tourists and even Ohio's governor, all anxious to get a taste of the family's cinnamon rolls, apple pies and good Amish cooking.

Valentine and Sarah Hershberger, the parents of nine children, opened their home eight years ago to a Columbus group shooting a commercial for the Goodyear Tire & Rubber Co.

During their time in the area, crew members wanted a place to eat near where they were working. Even though the Hershbergers weren't in the business, they decided to provide meals for the group.

"The workers started (work) on Saturday evening and left late Sunday night, and they ate here the whole time they were here," Sarah Hershberger says. "It (the business) grew from there by word of mouth."

The business, which has no formal name, is located off Ohio 651, in southeastern Holmes County, near Baltic.

One person who quickly heard of the Hershbergers' business was Lloyd Miller of New Philadelphia. He began bringing the Hershbergers busloads of tourists and business visitors to enjoy their family-style, home-cooked meals.

Breakfast at the Hershbergers includes: a breakfast casserole, home fries, ham, cheese sauce, fresh fruit, cinnamon nut rolls and bread.

Lunch or dinner includes: two meats, mashed potatoes and gravy, noodles, stuffing, tossed salad and four kinds of pies — apple, cherry, pecan, strawberry (if in season) or a couple of creams.

Hershberger begins cooking early in the morning for guests expected to arrive in the afternoon. If guests are expected to arrive by noon, she'll have extra help come in. She bakes the breads and pies first.

Twenty pounds of potatoes, a 15-pound ham and 10 chickens can feed a busload of 40, Hershberger says.

In 1995, an addition was built onto the Hershberger home specifically for banquets.

"Before we had the room added onto the house, we would place guests in a room downstairs and one upstairs, because we have a kitchen upstairs, and we would just run back and forth between the two," she says.

"Now we do business, Christmas and church banquets, too. Church groups from Cleveland and Akron will bring in their guitars and have a jolly good time," she says.

The business has grown so much by word of mouth that the Hershbergers now have two "step-on" tour guides — Joann Hershberger of Heritage Woods Farms in Berlin and Shirley Chumney of

Daughter Naomi Hershberger sets one of the tables.

American View Tours in Mineral City.

"The tour groups will contact the guides, and they'll bring them down here for around two hours, for breakfast and dinner, and shopping at the bulk food stores," Hershberger says.

The bulk food store, which the Hershbergers have owned for 10 years, is run by their neighbor, Clara Yoder. In addition, Hershberger says that her family makes quilts to sell.

"We've had visitors from Spain, Germany . . . seven or eight countries and I don't know how many states — Georgia, Tennessee, Florida, Iowa, Indiana. We have 70 (groups) booked already for this summer.

"Many buses are senior citizens, Avon representatives, Longaberger Basket consultants, quilters and last June, Gov. George Voinovich and his people came down, ate here and everything."

The Hershbergers host guests from April through October, Tuesday through Saturday.

"August is never very busy. Maybe it's because everybody's getting ready for school, but June and October are very busy," Hershberger says.

'Pie Mary' Just Keeps on Baking

By Rhonda Rosner

It wasn't just pie in the sky when Mary Yoder started her baking enterprise west of Holmesville about 14 years ago.

It's serious business for the 75-year-old Amish woman. On baking day, she begins at 5 a.m., and by late afternoon, she has produced about 50 baked goods — pies, cookies, brownies, a variety of rolls, bread and angel-food cakes.

Her renown for baking has earned her the nickname of "Pie Mary."

Even if you aren't hungry when you arrive, your sweet tooth will soon be awakened by the delicious aromas coming from the oven in the Yoders' basement kitchen.

"I was so old when I started that we didn't put up a bakery," says Mrs. Yoder, who has a private kitchen

on the second floor.

When she and her husband, Andy Yoder, built their home in the spring of 1973, she had no plans to begin a baking business. Quilting was Mary Yoder's vocation at that time. Her quilts were sold on consignment at a shop in Mount Hope. She was able to create 36 quilts in four years, six of which she kept.

"I could quilt ever since I was 10. I learned at home, and I could sew my own clothes when I was 12."

Baking replaced quilt-making when pain in her fingers made it too difficult for her to sew the tiny stitches.

Spring and summer are busy seasons for Yoder, who prepares pies, dozens at a time, for Amish weddings as well as other events. Cookies are probably her second-most-popular product.

Every day was baking day until some recent health problems convinced her that it was time to slow down. Sometimes she still bakes on Thursday, but on most weeks, her main baking day is Tuesday.

Yoder used to rise early — 2:30 a.m. — on baking day, but now sleeps in until about 5 a.m., she says. Baking continues until all the orders are filled and her tables are laden with a wide selection for walk-in customers.

She is assisted by her 15-year-old granddaughter, Marlena Yoder, and her husband, who helps out by opening cans, peeling apples, mixing the pie dough and watching the pies in the oven. Everything is mixed by hand.

"I don't bake as many pies as I used to before my knee surgery last January. I used to bake about 75 to 80 pies daily. Now I bake about 46 (items), but not just pies."

One hundred pies in one day was the peak of her baking career, she says. The pies were sold at a draft horse sale in Mount Hope. The next day, she baked another 45. The event occurs twice a year, in the spring and in the fall, and it is almost always a baking challenge for the Holmesville woman.

Sometimes baking for an event, like the horse auction, is spread over two days. It doesn't take long, she says, for two women to produce 145 pies if they make 90 one day and finish the project the following day.

Yoder prefers fresh fruit and ingredients. She only uses canned peaches during the winter when the fruit isn't in season, and she wouldn't even consider ready-made pumpkin mix.

"We make everything from scratch; we don't use pie filling of any kind."

Yoder says she never kept track of the amount of ingredients she goes through on a big baking day. Flour and shortening are purchased from a supplier and delivered about every other week. Because the

Yoders no longer raise chickens, they depend on neighbors to supply them with eggs.

Her bake shop gets more orders for cherry pie than any other kind, she says. A few raspberry pies are made every week, too, but these are more expensive.

Yoder also bakes bread, brown and white on alternating weeks, but each week, customers can count on seeing chocolate-chip and peanut-butter cookies and pumpkin bars. Her personal favorite is her version of Oreos — two chocolate halves with vanilla icing between them. She describes these as "the best you can make."

Although she says she could "eat a whole plateful of Oreos" herself, and she sometimes gets "a notion to eat a little pie," Yoder doesn't sample many of her own wares because she is diabetic. But occasionally, she will put back a couple of cookies for her husband and herself.

"We bake for the family, too, but not much for ourselves. We get so tired of baked goods."

Besides local people, her customers have come from as far away as California and Alaska. Usually the travelers are visiting local people who bring them to the bakery.

"When they come, they fill up before they go," she says.

Yoder says she has even received pie orders from people willing to drive from as far as West Virginia to pick them up. Some of her baked goods, such as bread, have been sent to Europe as Christmas gifts.

She doesn't know how so many people know about her; there's not even a sign indicating that there is a bakery in her home. Yet people come from far and wide, including some regular customers from North Canton who, on their last visit, stocked up with four pies, an angel-food cake, cookies and pecan rolls.

"I didn't think the business would get this big when we started. I don't know how the walk-ins started. People just started to come. Sometimes, there are as many as four cars out here at one time."

At first, her baked goods were sold through stores in Millersburg and Holmesville.

She prefers not to have her bakery pinpointed because she couldn't handle an increase in business, especially tourist trade, she says.

Yoder is a Holmes County native who lived east of Millersburg until her family moved to the Holmesville area when she was about 12. The seventh of nine children, she says it was not really her job to do the baking for the family, even though she learned the skill at home.

"We all baked. I made a lot of cakes."

Yoder says she warns her granddaughters that they "can't get married until they can bake pies." But with a grin, she concedes that the girls already know how.

She doubts that her granddaughters will continue the baking business. One teaches school, one is getting married and a third has another job. Only the youngest still helps in the bakery.

"If I feel good enough, I'll stay in the business as long as I can do it," Yoder says.

Some of "Pie Mary's" work

BREAKING HORSES IS A WAY OF LIFE

By John Roepke

The horse that wins a future Kentucky Derby might have gotten its start in Holmes County.

Amishman Andy Burkholder has been breaking and breeding racehorses on his Martins Creek area farm for the last 25 years, continuing the work his father, Dan Burkholder, started more than 30 years ago.

The younger Burkholder, 39, says he started breaking horses when he finished school. His brother, Henry, also breaks and foals horses at his farm, on the eastern edge of Holmesville.

"After I got out of school, I was 14 or 15, I started doing most of the breaking," Burkholder says. "Actually, I've been breaking horses for about 25 years. Breaking horses and boarding horses is my main business."

In that time, Burkholder has broken more horses than he can remember. There have been a lot of difficult ones among them. He's had his share of kickers and balkers — ones that will just stop and not want to go.

"I guess dad just started boarding horses, and that's how we got into raising the horses," Burkholder says. "We don't really raise them, we just raise them for other people."

Burkholder doesn't advertise; he relies on word-of-mouth for customers, which include both Amish and "English."

He estimates that he has between 50 and 60 horses, including foals, on his farm at any given time. The number increases during the spring breeding season.

Burkholder breaks racehorses or standardbreds, as he calls them. He also will break draft horses, the massive work horses the Amish use to pull plows and haul heavy loads, and mules. But mainly, he works with the standardbreds.

The first step, he says, is to get the horse used to having a bit in its mouth. Then, he'll put the harness and bridle on the horse and get it used to being driven. He starts by "line driving" the horse, walking behind it with lines attached to the bridle, so the animal will learn how to be led.

"Most of them I break for 30 days. Usually, by the end of the 30 days, most of them are going. They're all different, though. But most of them are going pretty good."

After he has done his job with a horse, it is returned to the owners, who'll take it to a horse trainer. Burkholder says trainers don't like to work with an unbroken animal.

Burkholder also raises standardbred foals on his farm. Horse owners from Cleveland, Columbus, Florida, Michigan and New York send mares to his farm to foal.

Burkholder boards broodmares, the horses that give birth to foals, year-round. When the foals are born, they are weaned for a period and then broken in preparation for a career in racing.

Not every broodmare will give birth every year, Burkholder explains, but he usually has more than a dozen broodmares that give birth every year. Broodmares can have foals for 20 years, he adds.

"They don't all get bred every year," he says. "I usually foal about 15 mares a year."

Burkholder has three standardbred studs; two are his and the other one is loaned to him.

The horse business is seasonal, Burkholder's father says. Spring is breeding season; breaking occurs in the fall. In the summer, the Burkholders do farm work.

The Burkholders have about 80 acres of farmland, 40 of which are hay and 25 of oats. They use the

crops to feed the horses, but they still have to buy some feed.

Dover veterinarian Dale Covy does pregnancy checks on the horses every few weeks, as well as performing other medical examinations.

Covy says a horse will carry a foal for 11 months before giving birth. During a recent trip to the Burkholders' farm, Covy found three of the four broodmares he checked to be pregnant. He expects those foals will be born early next April.

It is important to get the mares pregnant early in the season, the veterinarian says, because with racehorses, all their birthdays are considered to be Jan. 1.

The later a foal is born, the farther behind in development it will be compared to other foals, and that means a lot in the racing world, Covy says.

"The Burkholders are pretty good at getting the mares pregnant early in the year," he says.

MANY AMISHMEN ARE WOODWORKERS

By Kevin Lynch

There is nothing like obtaining fine quality products for a reasonable price. That is what makes Amish wood craftsmen such a valuable asset to the Holmes County community.

The Amish are noted for their fine quality craftsmanship, while the prices they charge are beyond compare.

Many Amish wood shops can be found nestled along the back roads of the county. They specialize in everything from tables, chairs and rockers to toys. There also are numerous Amish wood mills that specialize in pallets and other lumber needs.

The demand for Amish-made products is so great that several of the wood workers interviewed asked not to be identified because they didn't need any more business.

"There is no sense doing a story on my business

and getting me more customers. I have a hard enough time filling all the orders I have for jobs now," said one Amishman who makes chairs.

In his 31 years on the job, this Amishman has made thousands of chairs for satisfied customers from all over Ohio.

"I've got enough orders here now to keep me going until I'm ready to have someone take over the business for me."

The jobs come from friends of people who have had work done in the past or people who have had things built before and want something else made.

"Word-of-mouth is probably the most effective way of getting the word out about my work," the Amishman says.

The woodworking trade often is handed down from generation to generation, but that's not always the case. One Amishman began his career by helping his neighbor. Eventually, he took over the business and has carried on the tradition of producing quality, hand-crafted products for more than 30 years.

Because many Amish shops are one- or two-man operations, orders can take a few months or even longer to be completed.

"I'm almost ready to let somebody take over for me," one owner said with a laugh. "But not quite. I still need something to do to keep me busy."

Alvin Mast had been building furniture and cus-

tom kitchens for more than 30 years at his family run mill near Wilmot. But space became limited as his workload increased, so he built a new building.

With the extra space, he encouraged his two sons, Merle and Monroe, to carry on the family tradition of wood craftsmanship. They began producing hand-crafted wooden toys out of the old building vacated by their father, and the Wooden Toy Shop was begun in 1986.

"It started out as something for the boys to do, but it quickly became a very successful business," Mast says. "Business took off right from the start."

The Wooden Toy Shop became so successful that it moved from its original location into a large store in the Amish Door complex near Wilmot.

Abe Keim, who works at the Wooden Toy Shop, says poplar is the easiest wood to work with because it is very pliable.

"Oak isn't bad to work with, but it is a harder wood than poplar," Keim says.

The wooden toys are cut and mastered on various machines, such as generator-powered lathes and saws.

Most of the wood workers say their craft is something they have learned simply by doing.

"I've tried different cuts, but most of what I do is just from experience. I'm still learning," one craftsman said.

SECTION VI
DAILY TASKS

HERE'S WHAT'S COOKING

By Jean Stoner

Many things draw people to Holmes County — shops, scenery, craftsmen, to name a few.

And then there is the food. You know, it's talked about all the time. It's that good, old Amish cooking. People can make Swiss steak, mashed potatoes, noodles, dressing and all those goodies at home, but they just don't taste like an Amish-made meal.

Betty Kline, an Amish woman who lives near Holmesville, says there really isn't any secret to the Amish way of cooking. The difference between Amish and English cooking may be with the spices, she says. The Amish don't use as many.

Kline cooks at the Holmes County Training Center. She lives with her mother. Her sister and her family live nearby. Cooking is second nature to Kline, who serves about 100 students at the center.

If she has any cooking "tricks," Kline is not aware of them because they have become a habit.

"I sometimes use recipes, but mostly I just put ingredients together because I've done it so often. When people ask for my recipes for something, it takes a little thinking, and even then, it often doesn't come out right because you're not used to doing it that way."

When Kline creams corn, she browns butter in an iron skillet.

"I put it in a big skillet and brown a couple pounds of butter at a time. It needs constant stirring to keep from burning, but it adds a real good flavor to the corn," Kline says.

To brown flour, she melts a half-pound of butter and adds one-and-a-half cups of flour, stirring constantly until it's "really, really brown. Then I add water, beef broth, whatever, and it has a really different flavor."

Many meals at the Kline home are prepared with home-grown vegetables that are canned or frozen for year-round use. The garden is shared by the extended family. It contains many kinds of beans, beets, cucumbers, onions, sweet corn, potatoes, peppers and a whole line of melons. Tomatoes are Kline's favorite, and she experiments with the varieties.

"The big non-acid ones with no seeds are my favorite. They don't have a name, because years and years ago we got tomatoes from a friend and we thought they were so good. We saved seeds from them every year and start the plants in a hot bed," Kline says. "They are very meaty and sweet. They are late tomatoes, so I always buy an earlier variety, too."

Several years ago, a friend gave Kline yellow tomatoes. She liked them so much that she saved seeds from them and began growing that variety, too. She also grows cherry tomatoes and little, yellow pear-shaped tomatoes that "are as sweet as candy."

The Klines do a lot of canning and some freezing. Since their home has no electricity, the frozen food is stored in a food locker at a nearby town.

Kline's sister and her family raise beef and do their own butchering. The meat is shared among family members.

"We cut it up ourselves to freeze or can. When cold weather comes, near Christmastime, it's hog butchering time," she says.

While Amish children are in school, the main meal for an Amish family is served in the evening. When school is out, noon is the time for the heavy meal. When the men work away from the farm, their noon meal is packed. Breakfast is always a major meal.

Eggs, toast or plain bread and butter, cereal and leftover potatoes or meat are served.

"Breakfast is one of the main meals because it gets them started in the morning. The average family

bakes four or five loaves of bread at a time — some once a week, some twice," Kline says.

"Natural gas is available on many Amish farms, so the wood and coal cook stove is just about a thing of the past. We use it in the winter because mom hated to give it up. We'd miss it because it always provides nice and cozy heat. The oven is always warm, and you can stick food in so easily. But gas is so convenient," she says.

Coffee, milk and water are the beverages served with meals. The Klines don't have tea as a general rule as a personal preference.

Snack foods include homemade cookies because there are usually some around. They also like potato chips and pretzels, and a lot of popcorn is made. But ice cream is everyone's favorite — homemade preferably, Kline says.

The Klines don't have Swiss steak as it is served in the Amish restaurants.

"Most of our steak is canned fairly thin. We brown it, make a gravy, pour it over the steak and can it. Then we just heat it up. The steak we freeze is thawed and browned. We make a gravy and pour that over the top and put it in the oven."

Does she ever eat in restaurants? Not as often as she'd like, Kline says. She bypasses restaurants where Amish cooking is a specialty because "I get that all the time."

Amish weddings are a time of joy, but much advance food preparation is the order of the day.

Kline has helped with about 40 Amish weddings. Preparations start a week ahead with things that can be frozen, like angel-food cake. The cake part of date pudding can be baked early, too. Potatoes for potato salad and eggs can be cooked in advance. Celery can be diced early. Pie baking is usually done on Wednesdays. Weddings are generally on Thursdays, she says.

The morning of the wedding, chicken, meat loaf and potatoes are cooked. Usually, there are about 20 cooks in the kitchen, Kline says.

Asked why Thursdays and sometimes Tuesdays are the most popular days for Amish weddings, Kline replies that the tradition dates back to the old world, during the time of Christian martyrs.

"When the Christians were martyred, for some reason, Thursdays were safe because no killings took place then. Tuesday was also a fairly safe day. Because the martyrs lived from day to day, those times were happy when their lives were again spared. I remember asking my father the same thing, and this is how he explained it to me," she says.

Seeing the practical side of Thursday weddings, Kline says the first days of the week can be used for preparation. Tuesday weddings are more harried because weekend preparations are not easy and time is

short before the wedding day.

When Kline's sister was married, other relatives were called upon for recipes that would serve a large number of guests.

"So many pounds of meat and so many loaves of bread, so many potatoes and how many pies. You have to get an idea from someone who has done it before," Kline says.

"At weddings, the food is passed and everyone can eat as much as he pleases, so it's better to have too much than not enough. Whatever is left over is divided among the cooks."

The Iceman Still Cometh

By Kevin Lynch

When home refrigerators became common household goods in the 1950s, the old ice house went by the wayside. But in Holmes County, the iceman still cometh.

Marion Weaver, a resident of Benton, has spent the past eight years delivering ice to Amish homes where electricity is not used. Weaver is one of the few icemen who delivers ice to the Amish in Holmes County.

The burly 6-footer delivers seven tons of ice per day from his insulated truck to nearly 120 different homes, returning every four or five days, or as needed.

"I really enjoy my job," Weaver says. "I'm outside most of the time, and I get to meet all sorts of nice people."

Weaver explains that his truck is insulated, but not refrigerated. On a refrigerated truck, the blocks of ice would freeze together, making it hard to deliver to each home.

By covering the blocks with a large tarpaulin, he keeps the ice cold and slows down the melting.

"It would take three to four weeks for all the ice in a load to melt if the truck were left sitting in the sun," Weaver says.

He purchases the blocks of ice from Millersburg Ice Co. and sells it direct to the customers.

"It's quite a workout lifting the blocks," Weaver points out. Each block generally weighs about 100 pounds. "This job really keeps me in shape. It requires a lot of labor and heavy lifting. But I enjoy it."

Customers at each home on his route hang out an ice card to tell him how much to deliver. Wearing a rubber shoulder cover, he hoists the block and carries it from his truck into the home.

Weaver puts the ice in either an upright ice box, a chest-type box or, in some cases, a plastic cooler.

"It all depends on the sect of the Amish what type of equipment they will have in their homes," Weaver says. "Some families are more progressive and will have a modern-type refrigerator while other, more traditional families will have the old ice box."

The amount of each delivery varies for Weaver. If

the day is hot with high humidity, his customers will usually use more ice.

The average order is for a 100-pound block of ice, which sells for $5. Depending on the weather, he may receive an order for blocks of 25, 50 or 75 pounds.

In the winter, the Amish store their food in cold springs, so Weaver doesn't do much delivering then. He doesn't mind, however. He uses the time to go hunting out West and help a friend as a guide in Idaho. It's just another benefit of the job, he says.

Weaver took the job hauling ice when the route

An Amish boy wheels some ice into his home.

became available. He says there were about 350 customers when he got the route, but that number has grown to more than 600.

"I speak their language and that makes it easy for me to communicate with them," Weaver says. Having grown up in Holmes County, he is the son of Amish parents and speaks fluent "Pennsylvania Dutch," the Amish German-based dialect.

His respect for the Amish way of life has helped him get established with his customers.

"When you understand the Amish way of life, their not conforming to the ways of the world, you find there is a lot of tradition behind the blocks of ice," Weaver says. "For me, it's a pretty important job delivering to them, helping them maintain their way of life."

Family Relates a Typical Day

By Rhonda Rosner

The typical Amish family in Holmes County is often up and about the day's business before the sun peeks over the horizon.

Here's a look at one family's routine:

Eli Miller, 44, an Old Order Amishman, is the owner of Miller Hardware, located across the road from his home east of Winesburg. He begins his day at 6 a.m. and opens his shop an hour later. Even though the business officially closes at 7 p.m., the Holmes County native says he still walks around with the keys in his pocket in case someone needs something after hours.

He and his son, Wayne, 20, are members of the Winesburg Volunteer Fire Department and his wife, Katie, 44, is a member of the department's auxiliary. The couple's other children are: twins Marilyn and

Miriam, 19; Fannie, 17; and Jacob, 12.

Between 5:30 and 6 a.m., Katie Miller and some of the couple's five children begin milking the 20 dairy cows — a job that takes about 90 minutes. Son Wayne is in charge of the farming operation and taking care of the animals, which include pigs.

Assisted by her daughters, Katie Miller prepares breakfast, usually eggs and cereal. After the family has eaten, the youngest, who is exempt from morning chores during school, starts his trek to Winesburg Elementary School. The sixth-grader enjoys school, especially math and spelling, his mother says.

A snack is the first order of business as soon as he gets home in the afternoon. Then, he does his homework before beginning his chores. Any homework not completed is finished later.

There is no sitting around after the morning meal, leisurely sipping coffee and scanning the newspaper for these women. There are clothes to wash or homemade bread or cookies to bake. The family's current favorite is orange Jello cookies, Katie Miller says.

The main meal is served around noon and is typically a bountiful feast of chicken, dressing, mashed potatoes, salad and some kind of dessert. Supper, which is a lighter meal consisting of soup, sandwiches and fruit, is on the table about 5 p.m.

In the afternoon, the women occupy their time quilting, sewing and mending. Once in awhile, the

twins do some housework for neighbors.

Reading and playing board games are favorite activities after the supper dishes and other evening chores are completed. The children enjoy playing Clue, Phase 10 and Bargain Hunter. At one time, the girls were interested in crocheting, but the novelty has since worn off, their mother says.

In the evening, "it's time to sit down and relax a little bit. I like to read if I don't fall asleep," Katie Miller says, adding that she is "always busy with something" and has little time for hobbies.

Another pastime the Millers enjoy is visiting friends and relatives. Monthly visits to Katie Miller's mother, who lives in Winesburg, are family affairs that include her nine brothers and sisters and their families.

Most of the young people get together with their friends in the evening, especially on Sundays, to share a meal, sing and play games such as table tennis.

Many Amish families enjoy traveling, with Sarasota, Fla., and the New England states among their favorite vacation destinations. But for the Miller family, such trips are infrequent, Katie Miller says.

"Ten years ago we took the whole family sightseeing in Florida," Eli Miller says. "That's enough."

He didn't like it too much, his wife says.

The Winesburg woman says that she sometimes

visits her sister in Shipshewana, Ind., although not as often as she would like, and eventually she would like to take a trip to visit a friend in North Dakota.

Katie Miller says that the farthest she travels by horse and buggy is 15 miles — to visit her sisters in Fredericksburg and Baltic. She is accompanied on the two-hour trip by one of her daughters.

There is no regular shopping day for the Miller household. Because Eli Miller makes frequent trips to pick up paint and supplies for his shop, his wife sends her order along with him. But many Amish families go shopping once a month, Katie Miller says.

Most Amish in this area raise and preserve their own vegetables and fruit, and they even can meat. For store-bought supplies, they travel by horse and buggy to Berlin or hire a driver to take them by van to Wooster or Canton. Some of the products that the Millers buy at the store include mushroom soup, cheese food, snacks and ice cream.

Church is held every other week at the home of one of the members. During the winter, hosting responsibilities fall mostly on those with larger houses, and although neighbor women come in the day before to assist with the housecleaning and baking, the job of setting up the benches for the service is left to the family. The books and benches needed for church services are stored in a wagon and transported as needed.

A typical church service begins about 8:45 a.m. and concludes around noon, when the congregation is served a meal of homemade bread, peanut butter, pickles, red beets, cheese, meat, coffee and pie or cookies. Occasionally, a volleyball game is held in the afternoon and some church members stay for supper.

Because of her beliefs as a member of the Amish faith, Katie Miller rejects modern conveniences, but she says that neither she nor her children feel that they have "missed out on things."

Katie Miller says she has enjoyed her years of living and working in the area, and getting to know "almost everybody in Winesburg," because "everyone is a different person."

The Schlabach children: Heidi, left, Keri and Jeremy.

DEAR DIARY....

By Katie Schlabach

Katie Schlabach, an Amish woman who lives north of Mount Hope in Holmes County, kept a diary of her life for a month to share with our readers.

The Schlabach family is composed of: Katie's husband, Jerry, and their children: Jeremy Lynn, 11; Heidi Ann, 8; and Keri Leah, 5. The family lives on a 130-acre dairy farm — 60 for farming and the remainder in pasture and woods.

Sunday, May 1

Today, we were to church with the horse and buggy. We had around five or six miles to go. Each family takes turns having church at their house. One family has church one Sunday, then the next Sunday, they have Sunday school. So, we have church every two weeks. Usually, we get home from church

around 2 o'clock.

My brother, Marty, and his wife stopped in after church, so I quickly fixed supper in the oven. I made pizza casserole, corn, applesauce, frozen fruit dessert and cake and ice cream. After they left, we headed for the barn to chore. It wasn't too long 'til we got finished, but at least we had eaten. After chores, we all sat down and sang before bedtime. The children really enjoy that. We don't do it often enough.

Monday, May 2

We got up at 4:30 a.m. to milk our cows and feed the calves and heifers. After milking, I wash the milkers and dumping station, while Jerry does the feeding.

I have to be finished 'til 6:30, so I can fix the children's buckets and get Heidi's hair up. They get up at 6:15 and get themselves ready for school. They go to Mount Hope Elementary School. Jeremy is in the fifth grade and Heidi is in the second. Keri will start in kindergarten in the fall.

After the children leave, then we usually eat our breakfast. After breakfast, I did my laundry. I use a wringer washer with a Honda motor on it. It usually takes me around two hours to do my wash.

Jerry sprayed one of his fields that he wants to put no-till corn in. It will be the second year in corn. At 10:30 a.m., Duane, my nephew from Kidron, came to help around the farm. He works for us three days of the week. That works fine now, but I don't know how it will be during haying time.

In the evening, Duane started disking the field to get ready to plant corn. He used four horses. We have four work horses and one standardbred for our buggy.

The girls and I went with my mom to my sister's place to take things for a garage sale she will have on Thursday. The men had to get their own supper of veal sandwiches. I fixed broccoli and cauliflower salad, and they had cake and ice cream yet. After their supper, the boys played ball.

Tuesday, May 3

After I got the children off to school, I did my ironing 'til Jerry came in for breakfast. At 9:30, my sister-in-law came and picked up Keri and me, and we went to my sister's for a little visit. It was noon 'til we got home again and "Oh my, what's for lunch!" I hurried around and made home fries, eggs, toast and fruit and oatmeal cake.

In the afternoon, I made a batch of chocolate-chip cookies. I also stirred a batch of molasses cookies together to chill overnight and bake tomorrow. The children came home from school at 3 and are always hungry. They often get a snack of cookies and milk or whatever is around. We always eat super after chores,

so it isn't always too early 'til we eat.

After chores, the girls and I took Lydia with the tractor and trailer over to our neighbor's to take things for their garage sale. There is also a neighborhood garage sale on Thursday through Saturday. I guess this is the week for bargains. Lydia is Jerry's aunt — a single girl who lives in the house right beside ours. She works five days a week at Amish Door in the bulk-food store. She is the manager there.

We didn't eat until we got back from the neighbor's. There wasn't time to do much after supper but just shower and hike to bed. It's so hard since the time changed for the schoolchildren to be to bed on time.

Wednesday, May 4

This morning it started to drizzle, and it lasted most of the forenoon. Jerry was going to start to plant corn, but waited 'til noon. I did some baking for the bake sale tomorrow at my sister's place. I baked 14 loaves of bread and 21 dozen cookies. I did my laundry in the afternoon. It didn't dry too well outside, so I hung them in the basement tonight. No, we don't have an automatic washer or dryer. We just have to wash whenever the weather is nice or hang them in the basement.

Jerry planted six acres of corn. He wants to get the other six acres ready to plant tomorrow if the weather holds. Keri was outside most of the afternoon until the schoolchildren came home. Guess she got tired of my baking.

Jeremy often has a little homework to do, so he usually gets it done right after he gets home. He went outside tonight and did all of the chores and got the cows in all by himself and started to milk 'til I got out. Duane had left for home and Jerry was still in the field.

After I got out in the barn Jeremy wanted to know if he could go to the neighborhood schoolhouse to play ball. So, that was why he was more excited about the chores. They play every Wednesday evening during the summer.

Thursday, May 5

This morning, the sun was bright and it looks like a beautiful day. At 7:30, Keri and I were ready to be picked up for the garage sale. Dad and us girls and children went there to spend the day. There are five of us girls and five boys in my family. We had a pretty good turnout today in sales. But there is a lot of stuff left over.

Jerry worked in the field again in the forenoon. Jeremy and I finished milking, and Jerry went to plant more yet in the evening. He said he will eat supper after he gets in from the field. You think that is typical farmers, eating at 9 in the busy season.

Jeremy and I mowed most of the lawn after chores. Then, I also worked in the garden for awhile.

The girls were so tired after we got in the house that Heidi said she will take her bath in the morning before school. It's 10, and I want to wash my supper dishes yet.

Friday, May 6

Today, we had quite a busy day again. After chores, I did my laundry, then Keri and I, with some neighbor ladies, went to the Amish Door open house at the bulk-food and gift shops. They had a tent sale with everything 50-percent off. We got home at 1:30. I put things away and then did some of my weekly cleaning.

Jerry hauled a few loads of manure in the morning, then he biked to Mount Hope. In the afternoon, he finished planting his corn in the 12-acre field. After Jeremy came home from school, he finished mowing the lawn. We want to go over to Country Washer Sales after chores. They have their open house three days this week. They have paints, books, dishes and all kinds of things. When we got back, the girls ate peaches and cottage cheese, and Jeremy and Jerry had some ice cream.

Saturday, May 7

We got up early this morning, so we are finished

with the chores before Jerry and Jeremy leave to go mushroom hunting in Tappan. They left at 7:15. Two of my nieces came today to spend the day with our girls. They couldn't decide what to play, so I put them all to work for awhile. I finished with my cleaning, and they decided to play with their dolls 'til dinner is ready.

It started to rain while we were eating, so I didn't know if I could keep my promise of walking to the neighbor's at Country Washer Sales or not. But by 2, it stopped and we decided we could go. They had a drawing at 3. Keri and Heidi each won a door prize. Heidi got a set of 10 glasses, and Keri got a Rubbermaid wastebasket. They were tickled to get something even if they don't have use for it.

At 4, we went to start chores. It was 5:30 when Jerry and Jeremy got home, and I was just starting to milk. After chores, Jerry had to grind feed for the milk cows. It was a late supper of spaghetti and applesauce. After supper, Heidi and Keri went over to Lydia's, and Heidi decided she wanted to sleep over. I gave her permission. It's always a treat for them to sleep at her house.

Sunday, May 8
Sunday morning and it is still drizzling and very cool. Jerry drove Lydia to her church before Sunday school. The church starts at 9, but Sunday school

doesn't start until 9:30. Jerry and the children went to Sunday school, as I wasn't feeling too well. In Sunday school, we sing three songs, then someone has devotions. After that, the children, ages 3 to eighth-grade, go out for classes. We have three different classes for them. We don't have an adult class. Adults have chapter study.

In the evening, Jerry and I had a good rest while the children played ball. Later, Jerry's brother, John, brought his parents here for a visit. They just got home from Florida yesterday, where they live during the winter. It was good to see them.

Monday, May 9

We got up too late this morning, so I had to go wash the milker buckets after the schoolchildren left. I'm not crazy for that. It always gives me a late start with other things.

Jerry worked at the desk for awhile after breakfast, paying bills, etc. After that, he went and put the cows in the pasture. We feed them hay when we get them in the barn. After we are finished milking, he feeds them grain and later more hay. Then they have time to eat until after our breakfast.

At 10 a.m., Jerry and Keri went out to his dad's to look for our two heifers we had put in their pasture. They were at their neighbor's, so they borrowed a trailer to haul them back again. This afternoon they

put electric fence around their pasture. Hopefully, that will keep the heifers where they are supposed to be.

We had supper at Lydia's house. We had mashed potatoes, chicken, vegetables, macaroni salad, fruit, lemon angel-food cake and apple fritters.

Tuesday, May 10

Keri and I hustled around after breakfast, as we both had doctor appointments at 10 in Mount Eaton. She went for her school physical. The doctor is about five mile from here, so we went by horse and buggy. My sister-in-law, Betty Mast, went along because she wanted to go to Spector's Dry Goods Store.

Steven, Duane's brother, came this morning to help Jerry today and tomorrow. They are working on a project in the barn of putting in another beam. The old one is rotten. I didn't chore because the girls and I went to Kidron to pick up our leftover garage-sale things. We had a driver with a van, so we loaded things in the back of his van, and he drove it out to Save-N-Serve. When we got home, the men were eating supper, so I washed the dishes and read the girls a story. They often want a bedtime story.

Wednesday, May 11

By noon, Jerry finished the project in the barn. He put Steven at painting our new Martin's box before

we put it up. We have two other boxes, but it seems that isn't enough for the June Martins. We sure enjoy the Martins while they are here. Usually, they come the end of March and leave the middle of August.

After I finished the wash, I cooked raspberry and raisin pie filling for my half-moons. I want to bake yet today for our picnic, that is if the weather holds. I put tramps' food in the oven for dinner. You put a slice of onion in tin foil and slice a potato and carrot on top of that, and also cabbage if you have some. Then on top of that you put a hamburger patty and close the foil and bake it for an hour. They all just love it.

After dinner, I made 50 half-moons. Us sisters planned to go to Jerry Miller's woods for the picnic. After chores, Jeremy went to play ball again at the schoolhouse. Jerry had planned to go, too, but other things popped up and he couldn't go in time. We had to have a vet for a sick cow, and one of the work horses is lame and has to have his foot bathed. She was put on penicillin.

Thursday, May 12

Today is Ascension Day. We keep that as a holiday, and the children didn't go to school. At 8:30, Jerry Miller called and said they decided it's too cool to go down to the woods, but we shall just come over to their house to eat. So, after having our morning devo-

tions with the children, it was time to get ready to go. We still had a picnic lunch of hamburgers, noodles, hot dogs, potato salad, cheesecake and my half-moons.

In the afternoon, the children went outside and played ball, and the rest of us just sat around and acted lazy and visited.

Friday, May 13
After the children left for school, I did laundry and cleaned the bedrooms and living room until Keri got up from bed. That was 10:30. Guess she is all rested up for the day. Jerry went to the sprayer shop to get spray to spray his corn and some fertilizer to plant this afternoon. He stopped at the feed mill to get some medicine for our sick calf. We have one that is 3 months old and seems nothing wants to help her.

At 4, Lydia had a driver from work, and he picked up the girls and me to go to Mount Hope and stop at the greenhouse. I think I got most of my things now. So as soon as the weather turns warmer, I'd like to plant things.

Saturday, May 14
I got Jeremy up this morning to help chore. We got a lot of work lined up today. I baked a sponge cake and made Rice Crispy crunch bars. The bars are to take along to church tomorrow.

At 8:30, brother Marty came over to till one of our gardens. He wanted to demonstrate his tiller. He did a very good job of it. I want to plant my corn and beans in that part.

Jerry sprayed his corn that he planted a week ago and finished planting his no-till. It is soon time to start making hay. The children and I worked outside most of the day. Jeremy mowed all the yard, and I trimmed with the weed-eater. Then I planted some flowers and fixed flower pots that are on the outside porch. We had our first lettuce from the garden today, yum!

In the afternoon, I planted four rows of sweet corn. Jerry and Jeremy milked, while the girls and I washed off our buggy. I'm afraid our efforts were in vain, as it looks like rain.

The girls and I washed our hair and took our shower before supper. I just made hot ham and cheese sandwiches and root-beer floats.

Sunday, May 15

It rained on and off all day. I think my garden plants grew more already. We were all to church with the horse and buggy at Vernon Schlabach's. We have around five miles to go.

At church, at the beginning, we sing two or three German songs while the ministers go upstairs in a room to council and pray over things. There are usu-

ally three or four ministers. One has the opening, another one reads the scriptures. Then the other has the main part of the sermon. For the closing, we have prayer and another German song. Everybody stays for lunch of bread and peanut butter, bologna and cheese, pickles, cookies, coffee and tea. Everybody visits for awhile, and some help with the dishes before we leave for home. We often get home around 2. The church service lasts for three hours.

The people that have young folks give supper and have a hymn-singing in the evenings. There are between 50 and 100. Every Tuesday night the ministers and the young folks get together for Bible study.

When we got home from church, Jerry went for the couch and the girls and I went to Lydia's house. After that I took a rest, too.

Jerry and the children are playing a game of darts on the lawn. It's quite dark and they are still at it.

Monday, May 16

After chores, I did laundry again and Jerry finished choring and then started cleaning the milk house. I cut some dresses for the girls until Keri got up at 10:30. After she had her breakfast we went out to help clean the milk house. That was very much in need of cleaning. About this time of year, the milk inspector comes, and we want to be ready for him.

In the evening, Jerry ground feed for the dry cows,

and I got my wash in and ironed, and put everything away. I sewed a dress for Keri before supper.

The milk tester was here tonight, so I didn't help milk. But oh, my, it took them so long. It was 8:30 when they came in for supper. I made meatloaf and mashed potato casserole, peas and fresh garden salad. Lydia made dressing, so she brought some over and ate here, too.

Tuesday, May 17

I got some things ready to send with the mail after my morning work. I finished a dress for Heidi and made Keri another one for summer. Jerry made fence in the forenoon, and in the afternoon, he put up our new Martin's box. I want to spade out around it and put flowers in.

I baked and decorated a cake for Lydia's birthday today. We had a little birthday party for her after chores. The children went outside after supper and played "Andy-over." It was dark before they came in.

Wednesday, May 18

After chores, it was bustling around again to be ready by 7:45. Sister Clara and a driver picked Keri and me up, and we went over home to my parents' for the day. I helped mom spring clean her upstairs and closed porch.

Jerry had gone to the Mount Hope sale to buy

some straw, but it was too expensive so he didn't get any. In the evening, he came over (to my parents') and picked (us) up with the horse and buggy. Heidi got off the bus at their place at 3. Jeremy went to play ball at the schoolhouse in the evening.

Thursday, May 19

It was 42 degrees this morning. I think it was around 40 degrees every morning this week. I did my laundry after my morning work. Keri was in bed again 'til 10. In the fall, she will start kindergarten, so I don't know how she will get up at 6. Of course, it is just every other day that she has to go.

After I finished the laundry, I baked chocolate-chip cookies before lunch. Jerry went to Horrisberger Implement to pick up some parts this morning. In the afternoon, he helped me spade my flowerbeds. I planted some flowers again and hoed the new strawberry plants and the early garden.

When Jeremy came home, he wanted permission to go practice playing ball with one of his school friends. He went for an hour. The girls were helping Lydia do some outside work like washing off her sidewalk and watering her flowers. After chores, Jerry trimmed beside the road with the weed-eater.

Friday, May 20

After breakfast, Jerry mowed about five acres of

hay. He wants to put no-till corn in yet. I think the forecast is for rain until Monday. Oh, well, it will also rain on the corn fields and garden things. Keri cleaned the basement and one of the porches. I baked six loaves of bread. I bake most of our bread.

After lunch, Jerry went to our neighbor's to pick up his hay head to put on the chopper. Then I sent him to the greenhouse to get a little more flowers. After the children came home from school, they finished mowing, and I asked permission to use Lydia's mower and I mowed the inside lawn.

The fifth and sixth grades had a ballgame today, and Jeremy is all tired out. They played Winesburg. I can always see when he gets off the bus if they won or not. Yes, they won both games. Heidi was so tired she slept during chores and supper. Then when we were ready for bed, she was all rested up and didn't want to go to bed.

Saturday, May 21

Saturday morning and the children slept until almost 9. It's the only morning they can sleep in. After breakfast of cold cereal, I like a little quiet time myself. I read a chapter from the Bible and just meditated on things.

I baked a raspberry cheesecake and some streusel cake bars. I also did some ironing and put buttons on the girls' new dresses. Jerry and Jeremy started to clean out the hay mow for our hay this year. The girls also wanted something to do, so I asked them to wash off our buggy again. They did a very good job of it.

After lunch of beef with macaroni and cheese, I went out to plant my green beans and some more corn. Jerry finished mowing beside the road. After chores, Jerry and the children had a real ballgame. They sure enjoy it when Jerry helps them. After their play, we took a walk back in the outfield. We sure could use some more rain again to get the things started.

Sunday, May 22

What a beautiful morning. It's 60 degrees and not windy and sunny. Heidi went with Lydia to her church. The rest of us went to Sunday school. We had a carry-in dinner, so we had a feast. It was 2 o'clock when we got home, so we were all resting when some neighbor children came along home with Heidi. The quietness was past for us. I popped some popcorn and made lemonade. After chores, we ate supper outside between our two houses. I made veal sandwiches with cheese, lettuce and onions.

What a quiet and peaceful evening. Lydia and us just sat and read and visited for awhile, and the children were playing kickball and hide-and-seek.

Monday, May 23

I watered the flowerbeds and did laundry before breakfast. Jerry got the barn ready for the fly sprayer. He is a guy that comes once a month during the summer and sprays the barn and the front porches. We sure are happy about that, as it really helps. The flies aren't quite as bad yet because of the cool weather we have had.

Duane came down again this morning to help put the hay in the barn. He raked it up in the forenoon, then about 3, they started to bale it. Duane drove the horses to bale, and Jerry and Jeremy unloaded it. Guess I slipped out of baling. Usually, I do the baling.

In the evening, I helped Lydia mow the graveyard. There is a family graveyard on our farm, so Lydia takes care of it. She mows a few times in the spring, then some of the relatives take their turn, too.

Heidi got her first mailbox club back from the mail today. She was quite excited about that. She did her lesson and got it ready to send again.

Tuesday, May 24

We had a fresh cow this morning out in the pasture. Jerry and Duane went with the tractor and trailer to bring up the calf. The mother cow followed it up in the barn.

Jerry planted his last no-till corn today where we

took hay off yesterday. Now, he has to spray it. That is a relief once to have that on the side. We planted around 25 acres all together. We have about 25 acres of hay to do yet.

Duane took the soil out of one of my flowerbeds, and we want to put other soil in. The flowers never did too well in there, and we want to see if it's because of the soil. This afternoon, I cut the bathroom curtains and the girls each a dress. I want to make new curtains for the bathroom. I didn't have to help with the chores tonight because Duane was here until 6.

In the evening, Jerry went down to the woods and got some topsoil and put it in my flowerbed. It was dark 'til he came in.

Wednesday, May 25

After the children left for school, I washed my hair and then got Keri up. We were ready at 8 when my uncle picked us up with his van. We went to get my mom and dad and four sisters. One of my sisters has a birthday on Friday, so we took her to Dutch Valley Restaurant for breakfast. There were 20 of us.

After that, we stopped and visited my aunt who had a heart attack a few weeks ago. We then spent the afternoon with Ella, the sister who will have the birthday. We washed all her dishes in her hutch and cleaned windows. Some of us walked to a dry-good

store about one-and-a-half miles away. In the evening, our husbands came for supper. There were around 33 people. I think this is one birthday Ella won't forget.

Thursday, May 26

We had a thunderstorm and hail early in the morning, so I didn't start my laundry until about 10. I should have started earlier because then it rained before they were quite dry. I cleaned the bedrooms and the living room, and then when Jeremy and Heidi got home from school, we went out and started to work in the yard.

After supper, Jeremy went to one of his school friend's with the bike to stay overnight. Tomorrow is our school picnic, so they want to bike to school together in the morning.

Friday, May 27

Keri and I bustled around trying to get some eats together for the school picnic. Jerry hauled a load of manure and finished working on the no-till corn planter before we left. Now the planter is ready for other guys to use. We are finished with it, but we rent it out some.

It was 11:15 until we left home, and they were starting to eat by the time we got to the picnic. There are around 156 students, and I bet there were 300 or more people there today. It takes a lot of food. The rest of the day they played ball. Usually in the morning, the eighth-grade boys play the teachers. After that, the pupils just play until lunch. Then after that, the married men play the boys. Jerry didn't help today.

We stopped at Boontown Sprayer on the way home to get some spray things for the corn. Then it was time to chore. After chores, I mowed the inside yard and Jerry mowed some hay. Jeremy and the girls finished the chores and played "Andy-over." In the evening I read some in *The Budget* and soon went to bed. We were all tired.

Saturday, May 28

We were late getting up this morning. My, I don't like that if you have a lot of work lined up for the day. Seems this time of the year if you take a day off, then you really have to dig in the next day.

First thing Jerry did after breakfast was spray his corn. Jeremy finished up in the barn, then started to mow the yard, but when Heidi got up, she finished it. This year is the first year she mows some. She still enjoys it, but watch out until the end of the summer. The girls didn't get up until 9:30, so they should be rested.

I did my laundry again today. I don't like to have much dirty clothes lying around over the weekend.

Then I cleaned the basement, porches and kitchen before noon. The girls helped me with the lunch dishes, and then they walked down in the woods to play for awhile. I baked a cake for the weekend and put my wash in and put everything away.

At 3, I went outside to work in my flowerbeds. There was still one that I haven't put in my flowers, so I did that and put peat moss in all the others. I didn't help with chores — just worked on my project until I was finished. I came in at 7:15 and was a sight to be seen. I went to the shower right away and washed my hair before supper.

Sunday, May 29

Jerry and the girls went to church this morning. My back hurt, so I was afraid I couldn't sit that long. Jeremy has a bad head cold, so he decided to stay home, too. After the others left, I straightened up the house. I wanted to read awhile, but my eyes just dropped shut. So, I rested first before I read.

When I woke up there was no Jeremy around. He was in bed fast asleep, too. We should be rested for the rest of the day. A neighbor boy called and asked if Jeremy and the girls wanted to come to their place to play for awhile. Of course, they all wanted to go.

Monday, May 30

Keri was excited that the children didn't have to go to school. She is so ready to have someone home to

play with. This afternoon, Jeremy raked the hay and Jerry baled it. He got it all in two loads. I baked cowboy cookies and made rhubarb squares for supper. The children didn't know what rhubarb was, but we all enjoyed it. After supper, Jeremy tilled the garden and Jerry and I hoed the things that are up and growing.

I made some garden tea before we went to bed.

Tuesday, May 31

I worked in the garden until 9, and then it was time to get ready for my doctor's appointment at 10. The girls just got up before I left. Jerry and Jeremy worked on the hay chopper this forenoon. You should have seen them — they looked like grease monkeys. I guess that means clothes scrubbing for me.

In the afternoon, they cleaned out the machinery shed. That's another dirty job. I sewed a dress for Keri. The girls went to the neighbor's to play for an hour. Jerry and the children played some basketball after supper.

This is my last day of writing for this diary. Hopefully, you enjoy reading it.

The Schlabach family wishes you all God's blessing and a beautiful summer.

Section VII
Some Profiles

MOSE A. KAUFMAN

By Amelia T. Reiheld

Mose A. Kaufman lives on a beautiful hillside just east of Walnut Creek in Holmes County. His home overlooks the land he has farmed for most of his 75 years. Now, his daughters, sons-in-law and grandchildren run the farms, and Kaufman is the gardener for the Amish Home, a tourist attraction near Walnut Creek.

It's a job ideally suited to the gregarious Amishman. He admits that while he's not wild about the tourist concept, he finds the visitors to the farm fascinating, especially those from other countries.

Like most Amish, Kaufman does not pose for photographs, but he did make an exception once. He and a tourist from the Middle East had been talking about their respective beliefs. When the Arab put his arm around the Amishman and asked to have their picture made together, Kaufman agreed, "because I wanted there to be a bridge of friendship between Christian and Moslem. You know, there's just no reason for animosity."

Kaufman has welcomed a number of foreign visitors to his own home as well, many of them agricultural students from Ohio State University. He has traveled a good bit, too — to the West Coast and to Europe.

His library reflects his global interests. There are books from all over, in both English and German, and an entire shelf devoted to *National Geographic* magazines. "There's a lot of stuff in the world you don't like," Kaufman says, "but there are a lot of good people in the world."

When Kaufman was young, nearly all the Old Order Amish were farmers, and agriculture still forms an anchoring point for the Amish faith. As he puts it: "The man that lives from the soil is conscious that he is living under the hand of the all-wise creator."

The Amish population has increased dramatically during Kaufman's lifetime. And prices for both land and farming equipment have shot upward as well, so that it's almost impossible for a young couple to get started in farming without help. As a result, many men in Kaufman's church district are working in other areas, including construction, carpentry and

local industries.

It's hard to maintain an Amish lifestyle away from the farm, Kaufman maintains. He quotes historian Will Durant: "If you're living in an agricultural economy, religion flourishes, but an industrial society leads to a synthetic economy."

It leads to a system of spending and spending, spending money we don't have, Kaufman says. "I do not agree with that kind of bookkeeping. We will have to get our house in order someday because there will be a day of reckoning.

"In business," he says, "whether we like it or not, we're in a materialistic society. People get hard up and think they're not making enough money, but nature always provides enough."

In fact, the way Kaufman figures it, farming gives a better return than any other investment one could make.

"A businessman figures he's doing pretty well to make 30- or 40-percent profit," he says. "In nature, you plant one kernel of corn and you get a 500-percent increase. One kernel of wheat gives you the stalk for baling and two dozen kernels of wheat. Of course, it's not all profit.

"But nature does provide that way. I've often thought that you can take a gallon of timothy or clover seed on your shoulder. What you can carry on your shoulder can make you 10 big wagon loads of

hay and even more."

Amish farming practices have changed little over the years, but changes do gradually occur. Many of the Old Order Amish now use tractors, but only to provide power for machinery at the barn, such as grinders and threshers. On the land itself, they still use draft horses to pull the plows, cultivators and balers.

Returning compost and manure to the soil is vital to Amish farming practice, Kaufman says. Yet, "I'm of the opinion that the term 'organic' is a little blown out of proportion. We do use some fertilizer, some chemicals, but we try to use crop rotation and to get a lot of nutrients from manure."

Life on a farm has a comforting rhythm to it, formed by the progression of the seasons. Spring comes early on an Amish farm. With horse-drawn plows, the Amish are able to start working their ground at the first thaw, usually sometime in February.

"You can plow for two weeks in February," Kaufman says, "and keep on plowing through March. This makes for a nice, mellow soil and makes the work easier."

In April, the planting begins, with a sowing of oats, and then there's corn to be planted in May. By June, it's time to make the first cutting of hay.

"This is an interesting time of year," Kaufman

muses. "We have some fruit trees, and we've already started eating out of the garden."

In Mose and Mary Kaufman's meticulously maintained vegetable garden, there's a fine stand of rhubarb and asparagus, which are the first in a succession of produce to come to their table. Then there are lettuces, spinach and strawberries, then peas and raspberries. Although their peaches seldom escape a late frost, whenever there's a mild winter, the Kaufmans have a special bonus.

Throughout the summer, the vegetable garden continues to provide its bounty. Mary Kaufman spends hours each week canning and pickling, and giving away the surplus, mindful of the winter to come.

"Then you come into the nicest season of all, the threshing season," Kaufman says. Autumn is his favorite, with goldenrod blooming and apples ripening. "The fall winds blow through the trees, and there's a good supply of wood on hand — you couldn't take me to Florida then if you paid my way.

"All in all, living on a farm, planting and reaping, makes you conscious that all our sustenance comes from an all-wise, all-powerful creator," he reminds. "Having in mind where it all comes from makes you feel humble and thankful for the abundance of nature."

Alma Kaufman

ALMA KAUFMAN

By Amelia T. Reiheld

"The worst thing about growing up Amish," says Alma Kaufman, "was milking cows before breakfast." The cows were, of course, milked by hand, and pre-dawn chores were unavoidable facts of life on the Kaufman's eastern Holmes County farm.

"I just never was good in the mornings," she admits, although a hearty breakfast of eggs, cereal and bread thickly smeared with apple butter did cast a slightly better light on the matter.

The very best part of life as an Amish child was at the other end of the day. "There is a memory, a very soothing one, and I often return to it in times of stress," she says. "I remember as a very young child lying on the lawn in the evening, when all the work was done, looking at the sky — dad, the hired hand, the children, all of us lying on the grass, cooling off and looking at the stars."

Between dawn and dusk, the Kaufman family packed in a full day — farming, cooking, cleaning, caring for babies and looking after the livestock. From the time they were very young, every member of the family had a job to do, whether it was helping to feed the cows or setting the dinner table.

School, of course, was the primary occupation of Amish children between the ages of 7 and 14. But Kaufman recalls: "For me, school was recreation; the real job started when I had to get home and get to work. I hated days off from school."

With their lunches packed in pails, the children walked a mile down the lane to a one-room public school. Like their English counterparts, the Amish children took turns reciting their lessons, reading and solving math problems. They, too, played Red Rover and tag on the playground. When the English children went on to high school, though, the Amish children were finished with formal schooling, and were expected to take their places on the farm and in the home.

Little Alma was a bookworm. While other children chased each other around the playground, she'd just as soon sit under a tree with her nose in a book. When she had dishes to wash, there was a book in the drawer under the sink. When she was sent upstairs to air the bed linens on Saturday mornings,

she had a book — and a sharp ear for her mother's footsteps on the stairs.

"I had a running battle with my mother," she recalls. "I had chores to do, but I'd sneak off and read. She'd hide my books, but she was never able to put them anywhere I couldn't find them."

One night, her mother confiscated the kerosene lamp, but Alma finished her book — by moonlight. One of the best places for a girl to vanish with a book was the privy. There was an indoor bathroom as well, and Alma, the oldest of eight children, treasured her solitude, wherever it could be found.

Alma's teachers supported her love for books. There was a traveling librarian who came every six weeks with a fresh stack of books. After Alma finished grade school at age 12, she started going to the library to get her books.

"The librarian saw me reading books that were not going to be useful, and so she interfered. She directed me toward the classics. She'd send me three books in the mail — two fiction, classics and one non-fiction, usually a biography," Kaufman says. "I'd read them three times and then mail them back with a note saying, 'Please send more books.' She never charged me postage."

Alma thought she was pretty grown up by the time she was out of school. In addition to helping with a house full of small children and housecleaning, she took over responsibility for much of the cooking, especially for dinner and supper. The main meal of the day was served to hungry farmers at midday. Supper was much lighter fare, often served with rivel soup or fried potatoes.

Monday was wash day. Tuesday was ironing day. The women made most of the family's clothes, and, of course, there was gardening, baking, canning and needlework to be done. Fridays and Saturdays were for cleaning house, upstairs and down.

Every other Sunday morning, the family would dress up for church. The families of the congregation took turns holding services at their homes. The services began around 9 a.m. Alma's strongest memory of them is that "they were long and the benches were hard. There were at least two long sermons, and a couple of short sermons, with a 15-minute prayer period where we knelt on the floor," she says.

There was no Sunday school, so children attended services with the adults. After church, a light lunch would be served, and then the families would visit with each other. The children would play.

The Kaufman family never had much of a celebration for birthdays, but Christmas was truly an occasion the little ones looked forward to.

"It was the one day of the year we got all the candy we could eat. Mother tried to get us to eat breakfast, but it was a losing battle." There were oranges, grapes and other special treats. Each child received one special gift. "It wasn't wrapped, and you had to go look for it."

Alma's favorite toy was a rubber doll. And, yes, it had a face, unlike most dolls the Amish have.

"I always wanted a doll with real hair," she says. "My youngest sister was 13 years younger than I, and when I grew up, I bought one for her — one with real hair.

"I was a maverick," Kaufman confesses, when asked whether, as a child, she had thought much about the world outside the Amish community. "I dreamed," she says. "I made up imaginary wardrobes from the Sears and Roebuck catalog. I wrote stories, but never showed them to anybody. And like a lot of little girls, I even dreamed of becoming a movie star," says the woman who didn't watch her first movie until she was grown. "It was *'Royal Wedding,'* a pretty harmless film. I wondered then what was all the fuss about?"

Dating for Amish young people was rather secretive. The older teenagers and young adults would meet for socials, singing and playing card games in the evenings, and once in a while, there would be a party. A boy would send one of his friends to ask if a girl would accept a ride home in his buggy, and arrangements would be quietly made. The young man might be invited in to visit, late at night, after

the family went to bed, but Kaufman recalls that it was not good form to ask who anybody was dating.

"Parents might tease or hint, but probably wouldn't insist. It was very free, as long as both were from among the Amish."

Though it inevitably became general knowledge that a couple was going together, and parents would have been consulted, the first public acknowledgment of a special relationship would be when the couple announced their engagement — 10 days or so before the wedding.

Courting, Amish-style, didn't appeal to Alma.

"I was a feminist before feminism," she says. "I didn't like the idea of leaving my own name, and it seemed really stupid to promise to obey somebody who wasn't as smart as I was!"

When Alma was 18, she received her father's permission to go away to boarding school at Eastern Mennonite School in Virginia. There, in just more than a year, she was able to complete all of her high-school studies. She came home, and spent a year teaching at an Amish school in Wayne County. Alma saved her teaching wages, and then went on to Goshen College in Indiana, where she majored in history and English.

One by one, her siblings followed her example and continued their education. The Kaufman children wound up scattered all over the globe, with careers in

journalism, medicine, psychology, education, accounting and fashion design.

Kaufman's family eventually left the Amish community and joined the Mennonite church, but she finds, in looking back on her childhood, a great deal of value in her upbringing.

"I got a lot of responsibility early in life, and that was useful. Although it might have been nice to have a little more play time, having to work hard was a good experience."

There's much to be said for the simplicity and harmony of an Amish home. While Alma desperately wanted a college education, which would not have been possible as an Amish wife and mother, and although she chose to pursue a demanding big-city journalism career, she will always know the pleasure of quietness, the security of self-sufficiency and the warmth of a large, caring family — legacies from her Amish childhood.

Donald G. Beam

DONALD G. BEAM

By Amelia T. Reiheld

"Love not the world, nor the things that are in the world . . ."

That biblical injunction — from the first letter of John — one of the bases of the Amish faith, with its implicit simplicity, was the main concept that drew Donald G. Beam into the Amish community. From another perspective, it was also the very reason he left.

While it isn't uncommon for a person born into the Amish faith to leave that church and culture for a more liberal lifestyle, it's quite unusual for an "Englishman" to give up the accouterments of the 20th century for the discipline of the Old Order Amish.

Beam was living a life in the city that he characterizes as "incredibly fast-paced," when he began to read about the beliefs of the Amish. "I was more or less like a seeker," Beam says. "I was pretty much fed up with modern-day society. I sought a simpler lifestyle. I wanted a closer relationship to the Bible and to God."

He liked what he saw in the strict adherence to scripture as a basis for everyday life, in the family cohesiveness and in the simplicity of the Amish lifestyle.

Beam was perfectly content to live without television or radio, and didn't mind giving up his car. In fact, going about his business on foot or by horse and buggy seemed more appropriate, given his concern for the environment. In forsaking the distractions of the modern world, he hoped to find in the Amish lifestyle a stability and contentment that was lacking in his city life.

There was more to his decision to join than that, he admits, with a smile toward his wife, Miriam. He had became friends with Miriam's sister and her husband, and through them, he met the Amish woman he would eventually marry.

"I had to decide then, whether I was going to live my life with a lot of money and no real happiness. I've always been a simple person, and it just seemed to make sense. It still makes sense in a lot of ways."

Beam made up his mind to join the Amish church, and to ask Miriam to marry him. "I wrote her a letter and told her of my intentions, and then we had a talking date," he recalls. He then went to Miriam's father to ask his blessing.

Beam knew what he was getting into.

"As a teenager, I had my first introduction to Amish kids my own age," he says. His family lived in a neighborhood where the English and the Amish farmers helped each other out with the big jobs, what they called "neighboring." Beam spent a summer working on his Amish neighbor's farm and often sat around the kitchen table with that family.

"We were typical teenagers, I guess. You don't analyze too much at that age, but to me, there was no wall there," he says.

When Beam began to seriously pursue his interest in joining the Amish church, he began to find walls. Not insurmountable ones, but he had to address some real familial concerns on both sides.

As a child he attended the Catholic Church. He characterizes himself as a quiet, introspective sort of guy. Despite their kindness and acceptance of him, fitting in with a large and very sociable Amish family and community didn't come naturally.

"It's a very people-oriented way of life. My brothers and sisters were much older, and weren't at home when I grew up, and I was almost like an only child, so I didn't have that kind of upbringing."

Yet, Beam looked forward to becoming a part of

Amish society, with its stability and security. "I didn't need to worry that I'd get too boring for my wife," he quips.

Miriam Beam admits to having some misgivings because of the gap between her husband's level of formal education and her own. She finished her Amish schooling after the eighth grade, while Don Beam graduated from Ohio State University with a bachelor's degree in natural resources. Miriam recalls that her husband-to-be reassured her, promising that it was enough that she be a loving wife and a good cook. Besides, Beam adds, his wife is a very intelligent woman who can more than hold her own, intellectually.

Miriam's father, a bishop in the church, arranged for Beam to take formal instruction in Amish beliefs. Ordinarily, there are group classes conducted in German for the young adults in the district, Beam explains. Although he understood much of the casual Pennsylvania Dutch conversation, his command of the language didn't extend to grasping fine points of theology. As a result, he met with church elders who instructed him for several months in English.

Shortly after his baptism, Don and Miriam were married in the farmhouse of the family he remembers so fondly from his childhood.

"I couldn't have had a better wedding," he says.

Beam characterizes himself as a historian by

nature, and he found the traditions — with family and close friends gathered in the plain, old-fashioned surroundings — to be a very moving and memorable experience. "I thank the Lord that I was able to be married in that setting."

Beam invited several church leaders to preach at the ceremony, sermons (in fluent English, out of deference to the groom and his family) that focused on the importance of strong family bonds.

The Beams settled down in an old Franklin Township farmhouse to raise a family. Before long the two became three, and then four. Their sons, Jacob, 3, and Jonathan, 1, seem equally comfortable in English and Pennsylvania Dutch, unlike most Amish children, who don't learn English until they begin school at age 7.

Miriam has continued her work cleaning houses, and Don is in the business of repairing wringer washing machines, a job he supplements with horticultural work and carpentry.

"I do a little of everything," he says.

His dream, though, is to work in some area involving natural resources, ideally presenting environmental programs to children.

It was primarily his passionate interest in the environment that caused him to rethink the validity of his Amish beliefs.

"Love not the world . . ." says the scripture. And

yet, Beam does love the world. The way he sees it, the natural world was divinely created for people's use during their lifetimes, but shouldn't be abused or neglected. The Amish point of view is somewhat different, he explains.

"They look at our time in the world as a temporal passage, a pilgrimage, and we shouldn't get wrapped up or involved with worldly things."

Furthermore, he explains, Amish sermons emphasize their belief that the end is near. "Be prepared, for the end is coming soon," he says, "and if it could be today, why, you don't look too far into the future."

That purposeful ignorance of the issues facing the outside world, specifically, the lack of involvement with environmental concerns, became increasingly distressing. While the Amish way of life seemed intimately tied to the soil, the doctrine of detachment from the concerns of the world, without consideration for the future, created a conflict within Beam. His education, scientific training and natural bent had prepared him for a more active role in ecological issues.

"I'll be leaving my children behind in this world. I don't want to leave them a life of suffering," he explains. "I felt like I was in a cage. I was being held back, when I wanted to get involved in things they would ignore."

Beam finally decided to leave the Amish faith,

though he still feels close ties to the community. Beam says that "lower," more conservative churches probably would not have been as accepting of his request to join them, nor as understanding of his decision to withdraw.

"A lot of times, when someone leaves our church, it's on negative terms and they put the church down," Beam says. "In my situation, it was my own decision, and it wasn't that there was anything wrong with the church. I am still welcome to participate with them, but there's no way I could take communion."

Beam has shaved off his Amish beard and bought a truck, but the family continues its plain lifestyle. With her husband's full approval and support, Miriam remains a member of the Old Order church, and their children are being raised Amish. When they're older, they too, will have to wrestle with the dilemmas their parents have faced, make decisions and find solutions of their own.

Their future?

"I firmly believe they should have an education, but I'm not sure what they're going to do," Beam says.

The material attractions of the English side of their family will beckon, and so will the intimacy of Amish society on the other side. Beam says there's good to be found in both societies, but there's a special love

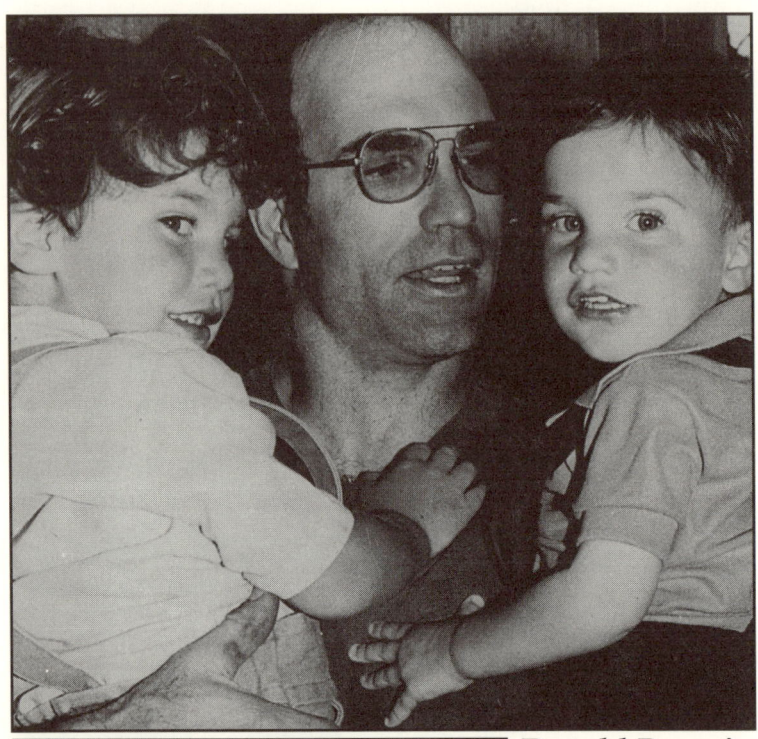

Donald Beam is pictured holding his sons — Jacob, left, and Jonathan — both as an Amishman and as an "Englishman."

within the Amish community that's hard to find outside it.

"On the English side, we were never very close. In an Amish family, it's always close."

Of one thing Don and Miriam Beam are quite sure, a belief that is fundamental to the Amish faith: Whatever does happen, it is God's will.

Section VIII
Conclusion

REMEMBRANCE OF THINGS PAST

By James A. Miller

On New Year's Eve of 1990, a Sunday, my Amish uncle died.

On that last day of the '80s the *New York Times'* lead editorial, titled "Faster," was making an argument for the decade's moniker as the Age of Speed.

Wednesday, into the '90s, the new and final decade of our millennium, I was among some 500 people at my mother's sister's husband's last earthly rites in Ohio's, indeed in the world's, largest Amish dominion. Speed was not, needless to say, of the essence here.

But questions of the "modern" and the nature of what it was to be alive in the last decade of the 20th century had never seemed so vivid.

The question is, "What on earth is there about the Amish that might be of interest to late 20th-century urbanites?" Some things are just too separate, too beyond the pale, too ahistorical to be of any real usefulness, are they not?

Oh, to be sure, eccentricity is valued enough in our society, though probably less in the observance than the breach. And as central a claim as any for our contribution to civic polity is a tolerance for a wide, even clashing range of beliefs, groups and individuals, just as the textbooks have said. All more or less true.

But really, this matter of riding in carriages as our great-great-grandparents might have — and did. Eschewing electricity, and so the whole panoply of modern accessories plugging into it as a generating source — television and Cuisinarts, VCRs and hair-dryers, to merely begin a list that could take up pages.

And the dress, if such it can be called: the made-by-hand, essentially uniform, essentially dark clothing, again of a vintage our forebears of a previous century might have worn — and did.

Horses, of course, both for carriages and farming; and so, no cars or trucks or tractors.

This just begins the list of distinctions and distinctiveness.

Interesting, puzzling perhaps, sobering or somehow bemusing, what is it about Amish existence in late 20th-

century America that speaks to anything compelling in our countrysides, much less our cities, much less our nation, much less our world?

A world that is the antithesis to all that this group seems to embody. All true, and all, as we might hope to see, somewhat beside the point; the point of their existence, too.

By the time we arrive, nearly an hour before the 9 a.m. funeral is formally to begin, dozens of unhitched buggies are already lined in rows by two sides of the barn. Which means several emptied stalls within the barn have a large and teeming herd of horse flesh milling about inside them.

A dozen adolescent boys — all dressed alike and only with difficulty it seems able to suppress the joy of their day's responsibilities — stand about as a kind of mobile hostelry to the families as they slowly come down the long lane and give their transportation at drive's end into their waiting hands. Their horse would be fed and their buggy recognized, each family knows, on their return, in some cases the better part of a day later.

Some who have come in cars, perhaps no more than 10 such vehicles, park in a field by the start of the lane, then walk down the sloping track as further buggies and hired vans with their Amish passengers inside pass beside them. A veritable pilgrim's

progress of arrivals.

A dozen or so yards over toward the house on two sides of the waiting boys are several clusters of 15 to 20 men and somewhat older boys (the women were all inside) standing together in a ragged row, silently or conversing quietly, altogether something like an unacknowledged receiving line for the mourners as they emerge, walking, from the lane or disembark from buggy or hired van.

Both houses, the larger main and the "grossdawdy," or grandfather, house beside it, are set up on a small bluff to the right on the approach. There, within, the rites of mortality, like virtually every other signal event in Amish life — birth and marriage, religious services and death — are to take place. As family, there is, in the hour before the formal service, a designated place for us, the nature of which but the slenderest idea is known.

Behind are the oncoming files and the groups of men. Ahead and up, the two houses, and no one, for some reason, is visible.

"Time's thievish progress to eternity" is the abiding theme not only of Shakespeare's sonnets but of every question of meaning, and indeed, ultimate reality. Certainly in this, the Amish are with all of us family.

Their lives, like ours, are ordered, however successfully

and truly, by their understanding of time and eternity. Their particular culture moreover is Western to the core, in that biblical grids undergird their unique history and existence; hence, time revolves finally around the God-man incarnated in history who both created the world and will in the end preside over history's closing.

This restatement of fundamentals is important enough in its own right — the basis for a linear sense of time supplanting the circular one regnant in the Roman and indeed the Eastern world — and apart from which, the Amish can be neither understood nor seen for the larger representation they are.

In the arc of Western history, an argument can be made, the group has, through some mystery of time-lag and resistance to the larger culture, come to embody many of the underwriting verities our culture began from, claims and disclaims, and not infrequently decries the loss of.

The Amish, in their degree of detachment from our time, might be said to be an instructive microcosm of a Western history gone by and yet, persistently and subterraneanly, very much present.

Several months before, in August, the "grossdawdy haus" had been the place where the better part of an afternoon had been spent sitting with aunt and oldest cousin around the kitchen table in the basement, where summer, to escape the heat, is lived in most

Amish homes, and with a half-dozen of her children, second cousins, roving about. The eldest daughter lived in the big house now, remembered from early youth; aunt and uncle, or grandmother and grandfather, lived beside them in the smaller house, passing over the farming as well to the next generation. Three generations residing almost as one.

With no one to direct us this morning, we turn almost instinctively then toward the smaller house, opening the door remembered, and we see in the sparsely furnished basement kitchen three somberly dressed young girls, who stand quietly to the side and gaze at us quizzically, even apprehensively. Thinking to help us, one volunteers quickly, "You can just go over to the other house where the service will be."

James A. Miller

Our imperfect but passable use of the "Pennsylvania Dutch" dialect (really, Deutsch or German) is convincing enough in the claim to family. Their eyes widen, in that look of familiarity and strangeness, and we are told, "Oh, you can go upstairs; they're up there."

The big December snow has melted, and yet its chill and the basement cool means that when the top of the stairs is reached and the door pushed open to a hallway, the sudden rush of warmth and the mass of humanity within brings instant blindness to one wearing glasses; lens cloud over in an impenetrable fog. In the shadowy dimness at the corner of each eye — only light from the overcast January sky illumines through the windows, save for one propane lamp — another century descends like a massive almost numbing blanket.

Closing the door behind and standing as if frozen in the warm hallway, with a room to either side, a sing-song, keening and indecipherable prayer is heard as if floating from a ground-level minaret in a further room, seeming to waft through the shadowy circle of rooms in slender, though ever-renewing waves.

Now with glasses off, to the right lined all along the perimeter of the room are the backs of dark, almost prostrate bodies bent toward the wall in prayer — a square circle of mourning and obeisance.

To the left — it could be seen now — somehow mistily illumined by the propane gas light is the open coffin and within it the glassy profile of husband and father, grandfather, uncle, cabinet- and coffin-maker.

After several minutes — no one can have known of

our presence — we find a place along the perimeter, joining a family, joining another age.

The Reformation, that great upheaval in what had come to be called Christendom, is the Amish defining period. The movement harkened back to the early church, whose "kingdom was not of this world" and whose members were enjoined to "be not conformed to this world," at the time of the pagan Roman Empire in the first centuries A.D.

The Anabaptists, or "re-baptizers," in this 16th-century turmoil ran afoul of both the Catholic majority and the Lutheran and Calvinist minority in their insistence on the separation of the true church not only from the "corpus Christianum" of the former, but from the state churches and the modern nation states of the latter as well.

Such a church could only be a non-coercive one. One couldn't be born, or baptized as an infant, into it. Only an adult, re-baptized as it were, could make a true confession of faith.

Massive persecution and death — decapitation and drowning, burning at the stake and other ingenuities — ensued throughout the numerous parts of Europe where the movement flourished, principally in Switzerland, Holland, France and what are now known as the Germanies.

"The Martyr's Mirror," a chronicle of this suffering, has stood for centuries, and to this day, next to the Bible itself

in every Anabaptist home. The pilgrim church is bred to the bone. Separation from the world was effected not only by the group, but by the world.

Over two centuries of conflict then — physically, entirely one-sided, as a central tenet was "non-resistance to evil," or Christian pacifism — and a mutually reinforcing estrangement found the survivors of Anabaptism scattered to the fortunes of the largely rural, less stringently monitored hinterlands of Europe. This was in marked contrast to the movement's earliest urban and university-trained sites and forebears.

In one such redoubt, the mountainous Alsace region in the border area of modern-day Switzerland and France, the tributary Amish line of Anabaptism was born late in the 17th century. The circumstances are less than clear in retrospect and certainly painful in many regards, but "separation" was again an issue, both between fallen or lapsed members and the group, and between the Anabaptist groups as a whole and the world. The question of "meidung," or shunning, is often used as a shorthand for the controversy.

Jacob Amman in 1693 pressed for greater stringency in this regard and effected, by 1697, a break between his followers, named after him, and the rest. Mennonites, the main body of Anabaptists, were so named early on after one Menno Simons, a dynamic, Reformation-Age Dutch priest who converted to their cause.

From their earliest days — in a persecuted Europe and then in eventual emigration to the New World (initially invited by William Penn to his "Penn's Woods," or Pennsylvania) in the following century and a half — to the hour of this reading, the concern has been paramount, negatively stated, to not be "unequally yoked with the world."

Who has not, group or individual, avowedly or tacitly, asked if not the very same, then a similar question: Where do I, and mine, end, and where does the world begin? And why?

The Amish, century after century, decade after decade, have given a very discernible, even defiant if humble enough, answer. An answer that to the larger outside world varies in its interest and appeal almost in direct or inverse proportion to the benefits and particularly the dangers of its own vaunted speed and touted modernity.

Several minutes before the appointed hour, the rooms of the "grossdawdy haus" empty in a single file behind the now closed casket, borne by six men, to the big house next door.

Another simultaneous service in another home is about to begin, too. At this very moment, an almost equal number of mourners will be filing into the neighbor's house at the top of the hill and across from the lane. He was known by many. They will all, at services' end, be returning here for the viewing and the meal.

Before the door of the big house, on the left, a line of 10 bearded elderly men, grim yet somehow kindly, shake hands with each of the family members passing before them, even the "Englescher's," as everyone non-Amish is known by. Yet, they know we are one of them, too.

A line of dark passing through dark, to conflate minutes later en mass within the warmth of the big house, and the service.

The Amish are like us, only less so.

One unexpected but instructive way to understand the 20th century is to think of it as a grand attempt on a massive scale at Amish life with machine guns. Socialism, in its millenarian forms, is an attempt through draconian coercion, that is, the brute, totalitarian force of the modern state gone amok, to fashion or refashion all of life and society in a manner both at war with human nature and the natural impulses of society.

Communism for the masses is as tortured and torturing an idea as is individualism for the masses. No such ethic or ideology can be dictated en masse. Reality lies elsewhere and will have its day. Only voluntary, non-coercive, pacifist if you will, associations can thrive and endure with a communal ethic.

The dream of communism for society as a whole is a

trembling nightmare of reason — the hellish barbarism of which a good part of this century has amply confirmed in oceans of blood. And the road to that nefarious abyss may or may not be paved with good intentions, may be with or without idyllic or deluded visions. It hardly matters to the dead, or the living.

The same ensemble of wooden benches that are moved from house to house every other Sunday for services now, in midweek, lines in close rows nearly every available foot of space in the two large rooms of the house. A stairwell leading both downstairs to the basement and up to a bedroom separates the two rooms, with passageway between the packed chambers on either side.

At the fore of the stairwell and almost exactly the center of the two rooms — the space is visible from either side — the ministers preside; at the aft, overflow mourners sit on steps leading up over their leaders, nearer than all the rest to their voices but mutually invisible.

The closed coffin is set against the stairwell in the far "family" room, which overlooks the farmstead. The immediate family (wife, children, grandchildren) is seated in the two center rows, facing each other obliquely, but angled toward the focal center of the dual rooms. Further family, in corresponding facing-

center rows, fan out behind them.

For 18 years he had been, as is customary, by virtue of being a coffin- as well as cabinet-maker, an unofficial "funeral director" throughout the community. Now, a neighbor and fellow church member is seating the mourners around his own plain, handmade casket. Through the near window, now propped half open to ventilate fresh winter air into the tightly amassed breathing within, the last of the mourners can be seen straggling up the knoll with a quickened step.

There are no formal introductions or openings, no songs, to lead. A tall, gentle-appearing giant of a man in his early 40s simply appears on the hour in the quiet at the fore of the stairwell, turns for a moment to face either room, and then, alternating his face between them, begins in "Pennsylvania Dutch" a noteless, lecternless funeral oration requiring no knowledge of the dialect at all to know and feel that an address of rare eloquence and power is being delivered. Forty-five minutes seem like 10.

A second homily immediately following, by an elderly cousin from Iowa, seems every minute of the length it is. And a third, by the local bishop, seems, no doubt for being third, twice its actual length.

Through the window a car emerges from the lane and stops by the barn. A neatly dressed, youngish

man with white shirt and necktie emerges and begins walking up the hill. In but this short time here, already, and strangely, he and his transport, indeed his entire world, now seem somehow alien, intrusive, even vaguely threatening. But all there know who he is and will recognize him. The local undertaker, as law and local agreement require, must be formal witness to the occasion; he would be there by graveside.

The bishop's peroration ended, he proceeds to read the obituary, first in the dialect, then, obligingly, in English; there are perhaps a dozen non-family "English" present.

Down the long lane — the view from the window again — and filing up the knoll, the mourners from the neighbor's house are arriving for the final viewing. In tandem lines, the men and women separately, a lengthening row of dark blue and black, hats and bonnets, they await in the January cold, then begin to emerge one by one at the top of the stairwell where the eulogists had been, and begin the stately circle around the now opened casket.

In this ultimate family society a loss such as this cannot be overemphasized, nor can the group's sustenance and support. An incongruous but somehow fitting and poignant edge to the final scene: the grieving widow standing by her lost mate and surrounded by bereaved children and grandchildren is physically

borne up and supported by her older, now "Englescher" sister. Family, if not every family member, dies hard.

The Amish have often been called a gentle people, and so, in important ways, they are. Their personal comportment and their way of life is in many ways in marked contrast to the harder, even abrasive and brutal edges of modern culture.

They are, indeed, gentle and loving, if firm, with their children; eschew nearly all the martial virtues in both their personal lives and with the world outside; and travel and flourish by antiquarian means and settings. Which in important, though hardly sufficient, ways defines them.

And yet, they are a hardy, in may ways stern, even implacable people, too. This is a view outsiders might easily miss by merely passing through their bucolic countryside, by their well-kept homes and farms, or observing their public relations.

A real cost, readily acknowledged by them, exists if separation and a "separate people" is to be maintained. "Ordung," or "Attning" in the dialect, the society's or the church's order and what distinguishes them from the rest of the world, making them Amish, is something mutually agreed upon by every adult member upon baptism, and it is twice yearly reaffirmed at communion services. In that context and within that covenant, an almost breathtaking,

all-encompassing body of support and sustenance is there and available for every member in good standing.

Major medical bills are paid for; barns lost to fire are re-erected gratis; provisions are made for unexpected, unavoidable loss of income; loans at no interest are available for worthy investments, particularly farming; "insurance" losses — in the mandatory absence of "worldly" insurance — are covered; fields are tilled and crops harvested, livestock tended, in the event of sickness. Mutual aid knows almost no limit.

But none of this is come by in a "gentleness" equated with sentimentality, or childlikeness, or naivete. The road is narrow and hard along their way, if filled with circumscribed joys. The broad path outside will lead not only perhaps to the planet's destruction, but, in far more immediate personal terms, to a shunning of those among them who fail to adhere to the many stations of the covenant.

Unless departure from the group is voluntary, till death do them part is a covenant made not only at marriage but at baptism, and it is equally permanent and binding — a long, slow climb to eternity.

The ground is slushy with the residue of record December snows seeming to lie very near the January surface of the field, as it slopes upward from the house to the plain, unadorned burial ground at the knoll's peak, a quarter-mile distant. The pallbearers

already have reached the site by the time the last of the several hundred — not all will venture the slippery ground — have stepped away from the lawn sidewalk and begun the climb.

No need for the long procession of buggies and the assorted cars; final earth is the cemetery at the hill's crest, rising between where all of married life was lived on the one side and, just beyond, youth. Though he might very well have traveled in his years more and farther than nearly any other Amish person, yet, finally, he barely ever left home.

Soon enough the attending group has assembled in a free-form circle within the neatly kept white and square wooden fence. The wind on the peak brings tears to some eyes; some hats are tilted against it; shawls are pulled tighter, defending. A mass of black standing at religious attention.

Suddenly in unison, at an unknown signal, all hats are swept from their heads. The waiting men begin. Two lengthy canvas straps are threaded on a board beneath the trestled coffin. Four men slowly ease the wooden box down. A further flat board is lowered down upon it. At this, the bishop, several rows back from the foot of the grave, reads aloud a verse from a 16th-century collection of Anabaptist hymns whose use the group has never discontinued.

The first earth begins to fall. An informal men's

chorus sings in unison the recited verse. Another verse follows, recited, then sung. Another. And another. The grave halfway filled, the four shovelers are relieved by younger men. Nearly completed, the older men again take over, shaping the sod. The verses have continued throughout, recitation then song. The mound is finished.

The bishop requests the Lord's Prayer, recited silently. A minute, several, and the first of the mourners — the last to arrive — have begun to filter back down the hill again as the others follow. It is over.

Only the ample meal at the house awaiting everyone and an afternoon of however long one wishes for visiting remains.

The community goes on.

The self is not sufficient, and as it negotiates its mortal span seems drawn to what lies beyond the hyphen following it. Thus, self-fulfillment, the modern dream, in its own way highly separating, stands in contradiction to self-denial, a central Amish virtue.

In this regard, "gelassenheit," a German word meaning, roughly, "submission," has been posited as a key to Amish culture, with submission, of course, a yielding to a higher authority, rooted in the biblical mandate to "obey God rather than man," or Jesus' words, "Not my will but thine be done."

The blood of their martyrs and their understanding of themselves as a church in brotherly community living in obedience — "a light to the world," "in the world but not of it," a "peculiar people ... called out of darkness" — has sealed their charter as a people decidedly out of step with the larger, speeding world, caroming its way from the centuries of the Reformation to our own bright and perilous day.

It's not "What's in it for me," the singular, reigning individual, but, "What's in it, or not, for us," the body of the submitted, living in community.

Those centrifugal forces of the age — secularism, individualism, rationality, gigantism, competition, relativism and fragmentation — have been resisted or wherever possible tamed at every step of the way and put to the service of the group by counter values, both unique to the community and yet shared by the larger culture, if held to less assiduously. The creation of this counterculture has been plainly several centuries in the making.

Technology and the pace of the world — the whole speeding course of things — are not in the saddle; the group is.

SECTION IX
CREDITS & MISC.

CONTRIBUTORS

The authors of the articles in this book were:
- **Jeanine F. Kendle**, who has been the editor of all six annual special sections on the Amish produced by *The Holmes County Hub*, of which she has been editor for the past decade.
- Current *Holmes County Hub* staff writers **Kevin Lynch** and **Rhonda Rosner**.
- Former *Holmes County Hub* staff writers **John Roepke, A. Nicole Springfield** and **Jean Stoner**.
- **Janet Williard**, a long-time correspondent for *The Holmes County Hub*.
- **Amelia T. Reiheld**, a frequent contributor to the special Amish issues. A free-lance writer, she now lives in South Carolina.
- **James A. Miller**, to whom this book is dedicated, was born in Holmesville and graduated from Central Christian High School and Cleveland State University. When he wrote *"Remembrance of Things Past,"* he was working on his master's degree in English. It was Mr. Miller's submission of his article that helped prompt the *Hub*'s first special section on the Amish. Mr. Miller died from cancer at age 41 in July 1993. He is survived by his wife, Lynne. The couple was living in Shaker Heights, Ohio, at the time of his death.
- **L. Edward Purcell**, the author of *"Life in the Slow Lane,"* is a free-lance writer and historian. He now lives in Lexington, Ky.
- **Leroy Beachy**, the author of *"The History of the Amish,"* is an Amishman who writes frequently about the history of his religion. He lives near Millersburg.
- **David Schlabach**, the author of *"An Amishman's Personal Expression,"* lives near Holmesville, in Holmes County.
- **Katie Schlabach**, the author of *"Dear Diary....,"* lives north of Mount Hope, in Holmes County.

The photographs that appear in this book were taken by:
- **Doyle Yoder**, who has achieved a national reputation for his photo documentation of the Amish way of life. Mr. Yoder lives in Trail, in the heart of Holmes County.
His photos appear on the book's cover and the following pages: 6, 12, 15, 23, 24, 47, 61, 70, 74, 84, 140-141, 144, 145, 152 154, 166, 186, 195, 226 and 250.
- **Ken Blum**, the general manager of *The Holmes County Hub*. His photos appear on pages: 1, 30, 54, 124 and 137.
- **Jon Kinney**, the editor of this book. His photos appear on pages: 36, 108, 101, 102, 103 and 104.
- **Mike Schenk**, the head photographer of *The Daily Record*, of Wooster, Ohio. His photos appear on pages: 62, 80 and 270.
- **Amelia T. Reiheld**. Her photos are on pages: 92, 232, 240 and 248.
- **Rhonda Rosner**. Her photos are on pages: 34, 150, 178 and the bottomm photo on 104.
- **Jeanine Kendle** took the photo on Page 202.
- **A Nicole Springfield** took the photo on Page 171.
- **Sue Politella**, a free-lance writer and photographer, now deceased, took the photo of Heinz Gaugel on Page 52.
- The **Miller family** provided the photo of James A. Miller that is used on Page 256.
- The **Donald Beam family** provided the photo of Beam and his two sons, taken while Beam was a member of the Amish faith.

ACKNOWLEDGMENTS

A number of other people also contributed to this book and deserve credit.

The project was coordinated by Ken Blum and Jan Conrad. Blum is the both the general manager of *The Holmes County Hub* and the non-daily division manager for *The Daily Record* of Wooster, Ohio, of which Spectrum Publications is a part. Jan Conrad is the general manager of Spectrum Publications.

Jon Kinney, the editor of this book, is the editorial director for Spectrum Publications.

Jeanine Kendle, in addition to being editor of *The Holmes County Hub* and the special Amish sections it has produced, helped immensely with the planning and development of this book. She also was one of the proofreaders.

Judy Wasson, a former region editor at *The Daily Record*, was the chief proofreader.

William I. Schreiber, whose book *"Our Amish Neighbors,"* published in 1962, provided much of the resource material used in two of the articles, is now retired from The College of Wooster, where he taught German for many years. He continues to live in Wooster, Ohio, and his book is still available at The College of Wooster bookstore.

Mark Olshan is a professor of sociology at Alfred University in Alfred, New York. Portions of an article that he wrote, "Should We Live Like the Amish," which was printed in *Christianity Today* in 1983, were adapted for David Schlabach's article on Page 7

FOR MORE INFORMATION

For readers who want more information about the Amish way of life, or for those who may be planning a trip to Holmes County, here are two resources:

• The Mennonite Information Center near Berlin in Holmes County (described in the article on Page 49) is open from 9 a.m. to 5 p.m., Monday through Saturday. It is located at 5798 County Road 77. The phone number is 330-893-3192.

• The Holmes County Chamber of Commerce can provide numerous brochures, as well as a listing of the county's motels and inns, and bed-and-breakfast facilities. The chamber's office also is located in the same building that houses the Mennonite Information Center. The phone number is 330-674-3975.

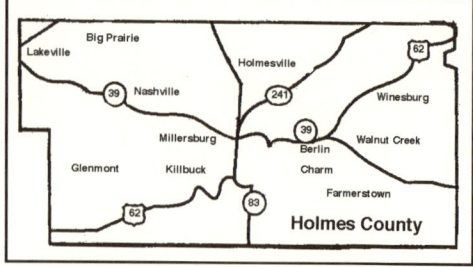